Christmas at Battersea

Battersea Dogs & Cats Home would like to thank all of the contributors to this book for sharing their stories and photographs

Christmas at Battersea

True Stories of Miracles and Hope

BATTERSEA DOGS & CATS HOME
with PUNTEHA YAZDANIAN

PENGUIN BOOKS

Penguin Gr

Pengu

Ontar

Penguin Ireland, Ltd)

Penguin Gr

Penguin G

Penguin Books (South Africa) (Pty) Ltd, Block D, Rosebank Office Park,
181 Jan Smuts Avenue, Parktown North, Gauteng 2193, South Africa

Penguin Books Ltd, Registered Offices: 80 Strand, London WC2R 0RL, England

www.penguin.com

First published 2014

001

Set in 12.5/14.75 pt Garamond MT Std
Typeset by Jouve (UK), Milton Keynes
Printed in Great Britain by Clays Ltd, St Ives plc

ISBN: 978-1-405-91970-8

www.greenpenguin.co.uk

Penguin Books is committed to a sustainable
future for our business, our readers and our planet.
This book is made from Forest Stewardship
Council™ certified paper

MIX
Paper from
responsible sources
FSC® C018179

Contents

Foreword by Paul O'Grady MBE

Battersea Dogs & Cats Home never closes its doors, even on Christmas Day. It will be there to take in any dog or cat, no matter their age, condition or temperament, as it does on every day of the year.

Sadly, the Home's kennels and catteries will also be full of residents spending the festive period without a loving home and my heart goes out to every one of them. Of course they will all be very well looked after by Battersea's staff and team of amazing volunteers, who will give up part of their Christmas Day to walk a Battersea dog or even foster a dog or cat in their homes over the holiday.

No doubt too that many kind-hearted supporters will send in gifts such as toys, knitted coats, and treats for the dogs and cats to enjoy on Christmas morning. Staff at the Home tell me that the Battersea postman, sorry, I mean Father Christmas, has also delivered some more unusual Christmas presents over the years such as party hats for the animals, a snorkel, a lampshade and even an underwired bra!

In 2013 Battersea took in 113 dogs and cats during the Christmas and New Year period alone. Given half a chance I would take them all home with me. But I must get a hold of myself before my home starts to resemble Noah's Ark.

If you do find yourself thinking about bringing a new dog or cat into your life over the Christmas period I urge you to consider whether this busy time is the right time and, like the people in the stories in this book, please remember the many thousands of dogs and cats in need of a second chance and give a rescue animal, who otherwise would spend its Christmas in centres like Battersea Dogs & Cats Home, a loving home.

As an ambassador for the Home I'm again going to take this opportunity to say that if you want to show your support for Battersea this Christmas, or any time in the year, by giving a donation to help the work they do, please call 020 7627 7883 or visit **battersea.org.uk.** The Home gratefully receives all donations and you can even buy their residents a special gift to help them feel some of the magic of Christmas.

Of course the dogs and cats don't know it is Christmas Day. Or do they?

Whatever you end up doing this Yuletide I'm sure you will once again love reading these tales from Britain's most loved animal charity and I wish you and yours a very Merry Christmas and a Happy New Year.

Introduction

In the small hours of one very special morning, young and old alike are waking with a flutter of excitement in their bellies. The morning sky is still dark and, although it's freezing, a tingle of anticipation is settling across every home. Excited children rush into their parents' room, while mums and dads sneak downstairs to turn on the fairy lights – and magic – for their kids. With good reason: this is Christmas Day.

But in and around London, an army is rising. At six a.m., Becky slips out of bed, gets dressed and quietly leaves the house. Her breath shoots out in misty swirls but, instead of frowning or shivering at the bitter cold, her eyes are sparkling and her cheery red Christmas hat jingles as she walks to her car. She turns on the engine and waits for it to warm up before embarking on a thirty-five-mile journey to work.

In central London, a man wearing a familiar blue sweatshirt heads outside and turns up the collar on his coat as he walks to work. Derek, like others on a very special mission this morning, will continue his journey across the capital, finally arriving at the gates of one unique place.

For many, Christmas Day is sacred, a day to be spent at home, sandwiched between hugs, sumptuous meals and presents. But over the next nine hours, one selfless team will set about giving the dogs and cats at this wonderful place the most special day. This is Christmas at Battersea Dogs & Cats Home.

At seven forty-five a.m., the overnight security team spot a familiar face approaching Battersea headquarters. With a buzz of the metal gate, Liz, a member of staff, is waved through and takes the gently sloping walkway to Reception. She is one of the first team members to arrive and open up. A jangle of keys, a swipe of a security card and she's in. Within minutes, the lights warm up from dim to full-on.

Soon, Becky also arrives and heads to the reception area of Lost and Found, where she works full time. She flicks the lights on and instantly the place is sparkling. The tinsel around the desk and the noticeboards shimmers, and wispy sprays of glitter add to the festive atmosphere now settled firmly over Battersea.

Becky checks the phone lines to see if any owners of lost animals have called. It would be great to reunite someone with their loved pet today of all days. She keeps her fingers crossed that it will happen throughout her morning inspection of the intake kennels alongside the team of rehoming and welfare assistants.

Over the speakers that usually deliver soft classical music to the various buildings scattered around the extensive site, a different type of tune now starts to play. Familiar Christmas melodies filter through to the kennels and cattery, while the air is filled with the aromas of cinnamon and nutmeg from festive embroidered scent pouches that have been sent in by supporters and now hang everywhere. Not only do the scents put everyone in the Christmas mood, but they help to keep the dogs and cats calm and content.

Across Battersea's three centres, in London, Old Windsor, Berkshire, and Brands Hatch, Kent, tails are swished and ears wiggled as the residents stretch, wake and shake off their early-morning grogginess. Before long, there is a flutter of activity as the staff and hundreds of volunteers walk along the corridors and set about their first tasks of the day.

In the kennels, volunteer Derek rolls up his sleeves, prepares a bucket of hot, soapy water and, after moving the dog in a kennel to the space behind it, 'the yard', he sets to work cleaning and mopping. In teams of two or three, the volunteers or staff members clean every kennel.

Across in the cattery, volunteers like Eunice, who has taken two weeks off from her full-time job as a nanny, are working alongside staff members to clean the cat pods and give the occupants their breakfast. Eunice takes one pod at a time, first checking to see what each cat is meant to eat, as some are on special diets, then preparing the food. Later today, they will all get Christmas treats, but for now, it's their normal breakfast.

Starting at one end of the cattery, Eunice sweeps each pod, changes the litter and checks that the duvets and blankets are clean, while another staff member or volunteer does the same from the other. Sometimes the cats try for a cuddle; sometimes they're scared. Either way, Eunice moves slowly and quietly so as not to frighten any fretful felines.

The kittens are another matter and like to jump all over her. As she delivers breakfast, Eunice squeezes it through the tiniest possible crack in the doors – inevitably one or two will attempt a daring pod escape to go for a snoop around the cattery. Today, Eunice wins.

Across each of the Battersea sites, the breakfast routine is also beginning in the kennels. Each dog has its own prearranged food, which has been individually prepared by staff, and volunteers like Derek deliver each bowl to the right kennel. Derek, a financial trader, does his best not to get attached to the dogs he sees once a week. He desperately wants a dog of his own but, due to his job and his rented London flat where pets are not allowed, that's impossible at the moment. At Christmas, more than ever, he feels the love a dog could give and would like nothing more than to offer one a second chance. One day, he plans to retire to the countryside and foster dogs in need of a home but for now he takes satisfaction from volunteering at Battersea.

Once the morning feeds are complete, the volunteers and staff in London take the dogs for walks around the sprawling site and across to Battersea Park, where the fountains are frozen and the grass is tipped with frost. With the backdrop of the London skyline, Battersea Power Station and the River Thames, it's a walk to remember.

Twenty-five miles west at Battersea's country centre

in Old Windsor, dogs get the treat of a winter walk around the centre's lovely fields and wooded copses. The rolling landscape is a sight to behold on the foggy winter morning. It's crisp and cold and only just daylight, but the duty staff and volunteers taking care of the residents across all the Battersea sites don't mind.

On a normal day, they might have time only for a quick hello to other staff who cross their path on the many walks that take place throughout the day, but this morning, with the centres closed to visitors, things are a little different. Festive chat is swapped and spirits are even higher than usual. Soon many of the staff will be playing Father Christmas as they deliver a gift, hand-picked, to each animal that currently calls Battersea its home. But first, at ten o'clock, it's time for a half-hour break.

Back in London, Becky of the Lost and Found office makes her way to the staff canteen for a cup of tea and a slice of toast. She can't help but think of how much her life has changed in the last year. She spent sixteen years working as a PA in the City of London before realizing her dream to work with animals full time at Battersea. Now, no matter how sore her feet are after a long day, no matter how many times her heart aches when she says goodbye to a special animal going to its new home, she knows she made the right choice because there is no other job like it on the planet. It doesn't matter to Becky if she spends Christmas at work because she loves the animals and is happy to be there. That's what everyone across the Battersea sites has in common: their passion for animals.

Before long, the break is over and Becky returns to her department. Other teams filter back to the cattery or the kennels to socialize with the animals and make sure they get a little TLC. Each resident is played with, loved and cuddled even more than usual. Many members of the public are very generous and buy the cats and dogs extra gifts online ahead of Christmas. They're spoilt with jumbo treats and a smear of their favourite snack: peanut butter.

In the cattery, the cats enjoy social time with volunteers like Eunice, who sits in the frosted glass pods and gives much wanted and needed pampering. During her time as a volunteer, she's learnt a lot about what the cats might want from their time together. Some like to be stroked and to sit on her lap, others want to play while a few may be a little bit scared of their new surroundings. In those cases, Eunice usually takes a spot on the floor and talks gently to the frightened cat. She'll tell them about her day, or quietly read her emails to the cat she's socializing. Sometimes it's that simple. The sound of her voice is soothing to the cat she's with, and it's also a calming moment for Eunice, whose family are in Scotland at this festive time of year. Often, for Eunice, spending the day at Battersea is the most fulfilling time of her week and Christmas is no different. Later this evening, she'll be meeting friends for a Christmas celebration, but now she's with her newest friends – the cats of Battersea.

Soon it's lunchtime and the staff gather in the canteen for a Christmas dinner of their own. But it's not long before the crackers and party hats are put aside. Now it's the turn of the animals to enjoy a slice of chicken or turkey, specially ordered in, so they too can have a Christmas dinner. They may not understand the significance Christmas holds for their human friends, but what they will know is that those taking care of them want them to have a day filled with love, care and special treats.

Meanwhile, across the site, the walkie-talkies in the Lost and Found Intake Office crackle to life. Liz, of the Lost and Found team, listens to the voice at the other end and says, 'I'll be right there.' She rushes to the security office to be filled in on the situation. As the guard explains that a shaking male dog has been found by a member of the public and brought to Battersea, she feels a familiar wave of emotion. *That poor dog could have been lost and alone for hours on this freezing cold day without food or water.* Sadly, it's a scene that Liz and the staff at Battersea have witnessed many times. Once more, she braces herself to pick up the pieces and start healing another broken dog.

Liz heads outside, and although she's trained to read animal body language and has had many years of experience, she approaches cautiously, slowly and gently, because the dog might be scared or nervous. He might also be injured or traumatized and lash out. That's why Battersea has expert handlers like Liz. Today, it's clear there is no danger, just fear and sadness.

7

The shivering dog is taken to the Lost and Found reception, where a nurse is waiting to check him over. She looks for injuries and illness, and when she's satisfied that he's all right, she gives him some water. He's still shaking, but every now and then, his body stills. The staff are extra gentle with him, and when their assessment is finished, they take him to a kennel with a padded bed, extra blankets and toys, and place him inside.

Becky is soon on the scene. With no collar, microchip or other clues, she christens the brown-haired terrier Pudding and enters his details into the database.

For the next seven days, Pudding is a 'wandering ward'. But on the eighth, he will legally belong to Battersea and can be rehomed.

By now, the shivering has subsided and Pudding is quiet. A late portion of Christmas dinner is served and he sniffs at it tentatively. Becky stays put while Pudding eats what is likely to be his first meal in hours. His water is topped up and, as Becky disappears around the corner to fetch something, Pudding lets out a whine.

When she returns, she hands Pudding a wrapped parcel. Jolly Christmas elves are dancing across the green and white wrapping paper, not that Pudding notices. He's already got his paws around the present and, with a squeak and a tear, his colourful new toy is out and his tail is wagging at full speed. Like every other resident, Pudding is receiving his own Christmas present; each one is carefully chosen to match the animal. The small terriers get tennis balls and squeaky fluffy toys, while there are heavy-duty, indestructible play-things for the bigger dogs that pique their curiosity and keep them stimulated.

Of course, no Christmas Day would be complete without turkey, a Christmas tree and snowmen, although here at Battersea, those items have found their way into the kennels in the shape of festive toys donated by supporters. Across the site in the cattery, catnip-stuffed snowmen and festive baubles are being juggled, chased and chewed.

By now, all the residents have had their presents and, after an afternoon's play, they are worn out. At five p.m. it's time for bed. The music is turned down, the lights are dimmed, and an hour later, calm has settled over the Home.

But before the staff and volunteers leave their posts and return to their own homes – and their own Christmas Day – they make up a few fresh kennels and pods, just in case.

1. One Very Important Person

I'd just sat down when a little face peered around the corner. Behind our Westie, Hamish, Lucky, our Collie, was waiting too, and their expectant stares were my cue to feed them. I got up and went into the kitchen. Behind me the *clickety-click-click* of four pairs of paws followed suit.

It was dinner time and, like an Olympic synchronized swimming team, these two were now moving in unison, but their sport was eating. Whatever they were up to, you never found one without the other. They adored each other.

It was only to be expected that Lucky would be the first to notice the change in Hamish. He had always been on top form, but over the last few days, he had become lethargic and quiet. Lucky sat beside him while he slept in his basket. Instead of snoozing, as she usually would, she was on high alert and moved at the slightest sound he made. Now, instead of being playful with him, she was very quiet. Like his shadow, if Hamish moved, so did Lucky.

I reckoned the recent cold and snow had taken it out of him, but when Hamish couldn't muster the energy to move and I had to carry him into the garden, I knew it was time to call the vet. Tests showed Hamish's kidneys and other organs were failing and, days later, he slipped away peacefully. He was fifteen years old.

Hamish had had a great innings but that didn't ease the pain of losing him. We were devastated and so was Lucky. A week earlier, Hamish had been bouncing around and now he was gone, leaving Lucky confused and lonely. Whenever she clapped eyes on me, her eyebrows shot up and I knew what she was thinking: *Where is he, Mum? When's Hamish coming home?*

After a while without Hamish, Lucky began to understand. She no longer jumped to her paws at the familiar rattle of the letterbox to race Hamish to it, and when five o'clock rolled around, she didn't stare at me with that demanding 'It's dinnertime' look.

I spent extra time with her, hoping she'd get back the spring in her step, and so did my husband, Jim. We gave her cuddles and kisses and tried to tempt her into playing with her favourite tennis ball. Usually she'd bring it to us, and sit staring at us with it in her mouth until one of us gave in, but without Hamish, she wasn't interested in anything, not even her ball. Lucky had lost her playfulness.

It made my heart twist. Lucky was only six, too young to be alone for the rest of her life.

One day I told Jim: 'I think we should get another dog for Lucky.'

He said, 'You're right, Anna.'

Although we said we were doing it for Lucky, there was another reason: we couldn't bear to discuss the emptiness Hamish's death had left in our home. Talking abòut it would have made it too real.

Day after day, we logged on to Battersea Dogs & Cats Home's website, looked at the pictures and read the descriptions of every dog that needed a loving home. We were supposed to take it in turns, but I couldn't stay off the site. I didn't know exactly what I was looking for, but I was certain that when the right dog came along, I'd just know it.

And every time I saw one that I thought might be right, the same thing happened: I'd call only to find another lucky owner had taken it. I was happy the dog had found a loving home so quickly, but yearned for a new set of paws in our house too.

Months passed, and autumn stretched into winter. In the mornings, the windows were speckled with condensation and outside the air was crisp. It was the time of year when Jim would go into the loft and pull out a box that jingled and jangled and was covered with glitter, along with our Christmas tree. As always, I set it up in our living room and slowly, bauble by bauble, decorated it. Every year I rotated the colours, and this year it was going to be red and gold.

While I strung on the lights and set to work with the decorations, Lucky lay down and watched me. She was so good around the tree and never got in the way. But I could tell she was sad. Usually, she'd come up and have a little sniff and explore the items now scattered around me. Looking into her soulful brown eyes, I sent up a Christmas prayer.

Please let us find a playmate for our darling girl.

Afterwards, I filled stockings for Jim, our sons Michael, twenty-nine, and Andrew, twenty-six, and one for Lucky, too. I placed them in the middle of the dining-room table and was about to go to bed when, suddenly, I caught sight of Hamish's empty stocking. I filled it with toys and treats and set it atop the others, just in case.

The house was ready when, three days before Christmas, a new post on the Battersea website caught my eye. It was a picture of a gorgeous, champagne-coloured puppy. I wasn't sure if a puppy would be right for us but I reckoned it was worth a call to Battersea.

I talked to the lady at the other end for a long time. Finally, I hung up and dialled Jim's number. When he answered, I told him: 'I'm going to Battersea tomorrow morning.'

He laughed. 'That's that settled then.'

We agreed to go with Lucky, Michael and Andrew, both home for the Christmas break.

I returned home from work with a printout and a heart full of hope. I showed Jim the puppy's details and read the short description again. As we ummed and aahed, I had a funny tingling in my bones. *This was the one.*

The next day, instead of preparing food or wrapping the final presents, I loaded Lucky into the car and, with Jim, Andrew and Michael, left our home in Kent for Battersea. Just over an hour later, we were at the Home's reception desk with butterflies in our bellies. I was

13

certain Lucky sensed that something exciting was about to happen because – all around us dogs were barking and chatting – she looked at me as if to say, *What's going on, Mum?*

We met Michelle, one of Battersea's rehoming team, and she took us into a meeting room. When we'd settled in, she said, 'I'll be right back.'

Lucky had a snoop around the room, then sat by my side, her tail swishing softly across the floor. She sensed something good was coming and looked at me expectantly every thirty seconds.

Minutes later, the door opened and Michelle was back. In her arms was a panting, beautiful ball of light-coloured fur. Two curious brown eyes stared at us through the most endearing black patches. The puppy had long legs and large paws, and was simply gorgeous. There and then, I fell in love with him.

'This is Cupid,' Michelle said. 'Cupid and the rest of his litter were named after Father Christmas's reindeers.' She set him down and carefully introduced Lucky to him.

At first, Cupid was full of beans and confidence but when he and Lucky took a whiff of each other he shied away. Lucky knew what to do. She went over to him and wagged her tail. She didn't crowd him. Instead, she hunkered down a bit and wagged her tail again.

That did it.

Cupid jumped up at her playfully and she raced back to where I was sitting.

14

Her tail was going ten a penny as she looked at us, then Cupid. I said: 'Do you like him, Lucky?'

Her body language told me what she was thinking: *Do you see him, Mum? Can you see him?* She padded back to him and it was clear she had read the situation right. Cupid was a bit scared but still playful.

As we watched them together, Michelle said, 'I don't think those two will have any problem getting along.'

That much was clear. And since Lucky had been my test as to whether or not we would bring a puppy home, she had sealed the deal for us.

She played with him and he played back. Whenever he got scared, Cupid would run along the wall until he reached a corner, then ducked low. There, he looked towards us with those gorgeous eyes: *What's going on?* The poor little puppy was confused, but the moment we spoke to him and offered a few words of gentle encouragement, he'd run back to us for cuddles.

Lucky persisted, too, and, though Cupid was wary, she was patient with him and, in turn, Cupid was lovely with her. Despite his fear, he so obviously wanted to be loved. Over and over, he flitted between us and Lucky, taking strokes and pats from us, sniffs and snuffles from Lucky. As he wiggled his tail and bravely tried to shake off the fear that gripped him every few minutes, the boys and I learnt about Cupid's background.

Cupid had been one in a litter of eight brought to Battersea days earlier having been rescued after they were abandoned. It wasn't certain if all would survive but Cupid was healthy and had been able to have his injections. He was ready for rehoming.

We learnt that he was an Akita, Foxhound and Staffie cross, hence his unusual handsome looks, and he was likely to grow to a decent size.

We might have been worried, but seeing Lucky and Cupid rolling around together, we knew it was a match made in heaven, and so did the Battersea rehomer who introduced us.

Cupid was meant to be our boy.

I filled out the paperwork and our sons helped put Lucky and Cupid in the car. While I drove, Cupid sat in the back between the boys and Lucky. Though I'd come prepared with a towel, in case he was carsick on the way home, he was a little star. Lucky was keeping an eye on him and mothering him.

When we arrived home, I pulled into the drive, and while Michael took Lucky indoors, Andrew scooped Cupid up and carried him. He set Cupid on the carpet in the hallway and Jim dropped to his knees to talk to our puppy. 'Wow,' he said. 'Look at your new home, Cupid.'

Cupid and Jim had a moment together, then Jim said: 'He's going to be a big boy. You know that, don't you?'

I looked at Cupid's gangly legs and laughed.

By now, it was late into the afternoon, and as the evening stretched out, Lucky was still keeping a careful eye on Cupid. As soon as he moved, she followed him. They played and rolled around the living room together and, suddenly, our home was alive again. I hadn't seen Lucky looking and acting so young in months. It was a joy to watch.

When Cupid played with Lucky, he still had a puppy's lack of control. He charged at her on his spindly legs and tried to knock her off her feet. When that didn't topple her, he pounced on her to get the better of her. Not that she minded. After a couple of hours, they were both worn out. As we all settled into the living room, we got to talking about Cupid's name. We wanted to give him a different one. We knew Cupid had some Akita in him and that the breed is originally from Japan so we tried to think of a Japanese name.

Michael said: 'What about Gizmo?'

I laughed. 'We're not calling him Gizmo.'

Andrew said: 'Well, what about Samurai?'

But Jim and I wanted a short one.

'OK,' Andrew continued, 'what about Sam, short for Samurai?'

It was perfect, and that was how Cupid became Sam.

That night, as Sam's initial excitement began to settle, he came over all funny. And he was sick several times. I picked up the phone and called Battersea's helpline and talked things over with a member of staff. She advised me that it was probably all the nerves and excitement of the day catching up with him. 'He should be better in the morning after a good sleep,' she said, 'but if not, call us back and we'll see what's best to do.'

We were on the phone for half an hour. Eventually,

weary but reassured, I wished her a very merry Christmas and bade her farewell.

Jim and the boys went to midnight Mass. Twenty minutes later, after checking on Sam again, I finally went to bed in our downstairs bedroom across the way from the kitchen. I tossed and turned and could hear Sam doing the same. He howled and whined almost incessantly. From experience I knew it was best to leave him to get used to our home, but I didn't sleep a wink.

Before I knew it, it was five thirty a.m., the time I usually got up to walk the dogs.

Unsurprisingly, I was the first up. Lucky, who slept in the bedroom, was excited to get into the kitchen and see her new friend. In fact, she nudged me to hurry me up as I turned on the Christmas tree lights.

Next, I went into the kitchen, where we'd shut Sam in using a piece of plywood as a gate. I found him in his basket, asleep. Lucky padded in and roused him with a big lick. As he stretched and yawned, I was relieved to see he was feeling better and hadn't been ill again in the night.

I let the pair of them out into the garden and, watching them together, I felt so very blessed that our new boy had arrived just in time for Christmas. It was usually Lucky's favourite time of year, as she liked nothing better than a busy house, and I was delighted to see that spring in her step. Sam was already giving her a new lease of life.

The boys soon joined us, and after breakfast, I put the turkey into the oven and headed to church, leaving my menfolk to watch Sam.

I returned to hear bursts of laughter in the living room. There, my grown sons were on the floor with Sam. He was jumping all over them and Lucky was playing along too.

I set about cooking. Every now and then, a wet nose or a swishing tail would bump against my legs.

When Sam and Lucky were napping, we sat down for our dinner but the smell of the food must have woken them up. Lucky was always well behaved and knew better than to sit beside us and beg. But Sam didn't have much of an idea what to do or what not to do. At first, he scurried around under the table, occasionally rising to his back legs and placing his head and paws on our laps. Each time, we gently returned him to all fours. But when he saw Lucky sitting and waiting patiently, he did the same. When we reached the pudding course, Sam had a lick of cream.

Afterwards, I went to the kitchen where the dogs' bowls were and called Lucky. She raced in and Sam followed, as I'd thought he would. I placed some turkey, vegetables and a dash of gravy in each of their bowls and they tucked in. It was the perfect time for the rest of us to get started on our presents.

Most years, that would have been the highlight of the day, but this year, the atmosphere was very different. Before long, Sam and Lucky had finished their dinner and were trampling over us and the presents. I fetched Lucky's stocking and the spare one I'd filled days earlier and, with Jim and the boys, helped the new friends discover their presents.

They both had a squeaky snake, and as I watched Sam bouncing over the living room in sheer delight at all the company and love, I melted. I'd always told my boys when they were children that you shouldn't get a pet for Christmas, but with Sam arriving hours earlier, Christmas felt extra special and it was all because of him.

Lucky was so lively and the two of them spent the rest of the evening playing tug of war. In between their battles, they chased rolled-up balls of wrapping paper and we all had a good laugh at Sam bouncing all over the place. With the two black patches on his eyes, he looked almost comical.

We tried to watch a festive film, as we always did on Christmas Day, but how could we when the star of the show was Sam? He grabbed our attention, and we took turns to play with him, unable to resist his adorable face.

Christmas Day revolved around Sam.

Every now and then, Sam would stop and take stock of his surroundings. It was as though he was remembering the traumatic first few months of his life, then wondering where he was and why this home felt so different from the others he'd spent time in.

At times, he seemed a bit scared, so we moved his little bed in front of the telly so we could keep an eye on him while we relaxed.

By the time night fell, and the more we cuddled, stroked and played with him, Sam's episodes of wariness faded as he realized we all had nothing but love to give him.

Lucky was exhausted too. Usually, she could chase a ball all day long and not run out of steam, but with Sam in the house she'd met her match, and by the evening, the pair were fast asleep.

Long before midnight we went to our own beds, tired and happy.

As the days passed, Sam settled in. He and Lucky became inseparable. Sam was easy to toilet-train, which was a blessing. A fortnight later, Jim underwent a scheduled surgery on his hip and had just returned home when something odd happened to me.

In the middle of the night, Jim nudged me. 'Can you feel that?'

'Yes, of course I can,' I said.

We looked down at my legs, as they twitched and jerked violently.

'My legs are doing the River Dance,' I joked.

But it was no laughing matter. I was rushed to hospital where a scan showed two discs in my back had burst. Though my situation was serious, the first thing I thought of was Sam. We'd only just got him and now I was out of action. How would we cope? Would we have to give him up?

It was a hideous notion: we were all thoroughly in love with him.

For the moment, I had to put that thought aside.

My consultant told me I needed emergency surgery to clear up the burst discs and fix my spine in place with rods. When I told him about Jim's recent operation and Sam, our new puppy, the consultant said, 'Don't worry.

You'll need to do as much walking as possible after this surgery to rebuild your strength. Sam may be the best medicine for you.'

It was such a relief, and with that extra knowledge, my mind was made up. We were keeping Sam. Having two dogs to walk would make me get up and about, and in the meantime, it would encourage Jim to keep moving and strengthen his hip.

My surgery was a success, and three days later I was at home. I couldn't sit, only stand, walk or lie down. To my delight, Sam took his cues from Lucky. When I took them for walks together, Sam paid attention to how Lucky was walking, leaving her lead slack and not racing ahead. It took him a couple of goes to get the hang of it, but with a few firm words, he was doing the same.

Although I'd initially been worried as to how Jim and I would cope, given his surgery and mine, things worked out well. The dogs were a blessing, getting Jim up in the night to be let out and making him mobilize his hip, even if he was using a walking stick, and keeping me on my feet during the day, relieving the pressure on my spine. Which was just as well: long after Jim had healed and gone back to work, I still couldn't tolerate sitting. It kept me off work and, without Lucky and Sam to keep me company, I would have been very lonely indeed.

Between playing in the garden and our long walks in the morning and evening, Lucky showed Sam the ropes. As a puppy, she'd chewed through everything, including a Persian carpet, but Sam seemed to know not to do that, and if he ever had a destructive moment, Lucky would stop him.

When she went out into the garden, Sam followed. She taught him to fetch the ball when we threw it and bring it back to us. Sam learnt it was nicer to play on the grass and stayed off the patio, where our outdoor furniture was, by following Lucky: she stuck to the softer areas.

Some things about Sam rubbed off on Lucky, and that wasn't so good. She began to display some defensive traits when her comrade in arms was around. I could see the two of them were becoming a bit too boisterous when they were together so I had to remind Lucky that she couldn't behave like that. We went through a phase when I was telling Lucky off a lot for being a bit naughty, but it didn't last long.

Lucky and Sam were the best of friends. They tore round the house together, chasing each other this way and that before collapsing in a heap and taking a well-earned rest.

As Sam grew bigger and stronger, he became pushy with Lucky. She tolerated his behaviour, like a big sister putting up with her sometimes annoying (not so) little brother.

At nap times, Sam would shove Lucky out of her much-smaller bed and jam himself into it. Lucky would gruffly pad over to Sam's before resuming her nap. It was a nuisance, but she didn't fight him over it: she simply sacrificed her spot.

In the evenings, when I gave them identical treats, Sam would drop his and grab Lucky's out of her mouth. At first, she let go of hers and picked up his instead. I told Sam off in the beginning but then I noticed something. As the battle for treats continued, Lucky and Sam made it into a game. Instead of relinquishing her treat, Lucky clamped her jaw and, with the treat sticking out of her mouth, tried to tempt Sam with it. He'd drop his and make a beeline for hers and the two would tussle, her growling, him whining, before Lucky gave in.

It was a fun game they both enjoyed so I left them to it. It was wonderful to see Lucky being playful and having a good time again. Who was I to break up their games?

Lucky was her old self. Her tail was constantly upright, she was lively and excited once more to go for walks and play in the garden.

When we took them out together, people would stop and ask to take pictures of our gorgeous Sam. Trying to get him to keep still long enough wasn't easy. He was so nosy and was straight in there, sniffing at his admirers and investigating their cameras.

As he grew bigger and older, he developed a bit of a dominant streak, as was to be expected of an Akita cross. We set him up for doggy daycare once a week to get him used to other dogs of different sizes. It did the trick. But some of his Akita personality would never change. Whenever there was a knock at the door, Lucky would bark and race to it, telling us keenly: *Someone is here!* Sam's method was different. He hung back until the visitor was in the house and he was close enough to check them out. Sometimes he'd get frustrated with Lucky and nudge her to be quiet. I'm sure he told Lucky many times in his own way: *Wait a minute, Lucky. Let's see what's happening before we get stuck in.*

He was much more of a guard dog, waiting to analyse the situation before acting.

So, between Lucky's fearless approach and Sam's natural wariness, Jim and I felt in safe hands. We knew if a burglar braved Lucky's barking to get into our home, Sam would give them an unexpected fright once they were there.

As for friends and family who came to our home, Lucky's excitement at seeing the familiar faces rubbed off on Sam. He took his cue from her and it was a tough job getting them to calm down. As time went on, Sam stopped taking his cues from Lucky and became his own man about the house.

Deep down, he was a softie and very intuitive. He was wary, and I guessed it was because of his breed. I reckoned that trait was likely to stay with him for ever. When we were out walking, if somebody was behind us, Sam kept one eye on them, one on the road ahead.

He also had a way of making other people confront their fears too, albeit without permission. Whenever my brother Arthur, who was terrified of dogs, plucked up enough courage to visit, Sam was oblivious to his nerves. As soon as he arrived, Sam would bound up to him and promptly take a seat on his lap. As the months passed and he grew heavier, he didn't seem to grasp how big he was. He had no self-awareness. He became a stocky dog with lots of opinions. He'd tell you about his day, howl and chat. And if he wanted something, boy, would you know it!

Lucky didn't let Sam push her around and, though she was 20 kilos to his 37.5, she wasn't afraid of him. In fact, we had to tell her off for inciting Sam to go on the hunt for squirrels in the garden. She knew he would follow her lead, and when she wanted to, she got him into trouble.

It was a good thing Lucky was tolerant because Sam was protective but rough. When he was still a puppy he would nudge her this way and that, but when he'd grown up, he'd gallop over to her and throw himself on to her. That was how their friendship worked. We discovered that, as long as Sam had a toy in his mouth, like his favourite squeaky snake, they could run about together and be safe. The only time they came to blows was if Sam got too excited and didn't have that snake nearby. Then he'd have a nibble at Lucky. She'd get annoyed and shy away. Sam would quickly realize he'd upset her and calm down until he'd won her over.

Although he could get on her nerves, he would never let any harm come to her.

Once we were in the park and a feisty dog came over, trying to get at Lucky. Sam didn't growl or bark. He simply blocked it. Over and over, he stood between that dog and Lucky.

Sometimes his lack of self-awareness got the better of him. He loved playing with small dogs, which we put down to his happy relationship with Lucky. We found, though, that he wasn't able to run around with them. He was too big and ended up bowling them over. After that had happened a few times, we kept him on a lead unless there weren't any small dogs about. When bigger dogs were around, Sam had a tendency to growl. We told him off and, on the whole, he was all right. Once he was attacked by another big dog and, though he's not usually aggressive, he defended himself.

Afterwards, it quickly became apparent that the fight had shaken him. Whenever he saw a big black dog, like the one that had got the better of him in the park, he'd have a shout and become aggressive. So, once a week, we sent him for a walk with a dog-walker, Steve, who took seven others with them. That problem was soon sorted out.

I learnt Sam was protective of me, too, and I reckoned that was the Akita in him. He had the stubborn and determined spirit seen in the breed. And though he had a tendency to be a bit aloof, he was very switched on when it mattered. Sam took a shine to some people, like my brother Arthur, and let them pet him straight away. There were others that he wouldn't let near him.

One summer's night, Jim and I took him for a walk, and on the way we passed a pub. It was a warm Saturday night and two guys were leaving on their way home. They were a bit the worse for wear, but when they saw us and Sam, they began chatting to us and telling us how beautiful Sam was.

Jim and I told them about Sam coming from

Battersea Dogs & Cats Home, and they were fascinated by his story. But while we were talking, I became aware of something. They kept trying to pet Sam, but never seemed to connect with his fur. It wasn't because they were so drunk that they were aiming incorrectly but because Sam was dodging their advances. He obviously hadn't liked the look of them and was avoiding them. I reckoned Sam could tell they were drunk.

After a few minutes, Jim had spotted it too and both of us held back a laugh when our eyes met. Afterwards Jim told Sam, 'You're a smart boy.' Sam gave a wag of his tail and went back to his walk.

The following Christmas, Lucky and Sam bounced around as I set up the tree and repeated our usual Christmas routine. That year, Sam got a bigger squeaky snake – he still carries it in his mouth at some point during most days.

Now he is two and a half and still bounds around like a puppy. Like most dogs, he'll do anything for a treat, and if you keep him waiting, he'll let out a yawn that stretches into chatter. Usually, that's his way of saying: *Come on, then!*

Both Lucky and Sam have a basket in the bedroom with us now but the door is usually open and they go upstairs to the boys' rooms whenever they're home. Where one goes, the other usually follows, and it's lovely seeing the bond the two of them share.

After Hamish, Sam is the best thing that could have happened to Lucky. She thinks so too.

The other week, Michael came home after two weeks

away and wanted to say a proper hello first to Lucky, who had previously been very much his dog. He took her into the conservatory and shut the door to have a cuddle and give her some one-to-one attention.

Lucky wasn't having any of it. She was pawing at the door and looking to Michael to act. She was telling him: *Let him in, let him in, LET SAM IN!* She loves Sam so much she can't bear to be apart from him, if only for a few minutes.

It's no wonder that Sam thinks he's a VIP. He struts about the house and commands everybody's attention. And, in truth, he is very important . . . to me, to Jim and most of all to Lucky.

Though, even now, Lucky still checks every Westie we meet, just to see if it's Hamish. If we say his name, Lucky looks at us with the same question on her face: *Where is he?*

That's why it's so important that we brought Sam into our home and made him a part of our family.

Without Battersea, that would never have happened. They have such an excellent attitude towards helping the animals, and they were first class in helping us. The key for us was being honest about what we were looking for, and Battersea helped us find that special dog to be friends with Lucky. That initial meeting, to introduce Lucky to Sam, was the most vital part of our journey.

Now Sam is the biggest personality in the house. He hogs the sofa and howls at us when we don't listen to him. But he is *our* Sam and we wouldn't change him for the world.

2. Faith, Hope and Survival

A Shocking Discovery

Every Tuesday, I pulled on a familiar blue shirt and headed off to Battersea Dogs & Cats Home in Old Windsor. I had lived in Greece for many years, working with street and rescue dogs, then moved to the UK with my husband. When we arrived, I missed my work so much that my husband said: 'Helle, why don't you do some volunteer work with Battersea Dogs & Cats Home?'

He'd planted the seed, and now my work as a volunteer at Battersea was my favourite time of the week. I was a dog walker and socializer at the Home, a dream come true: I loved working with particularly big or difficult dogs. I had completed my training, which enabled me to walk even the most challenging dogs, including those on behaviour programmes, and help them on their journey through the Home. I loved it.

A particular favourite was a girl named Foxy. She was a lovely Akita but, for some sad reason, she'd been waiting for a new family for more than ten months. I took her for a walk every week and got to know her well. She was a reserved dog, as Akitas often are by nature, and especially so around men. But when she got to know you, she was very playful and affectionate. Once she'd let you into her world, she was funny, sweet and quick to learn.

So, on Tuesdays, Foxy was usually the first I'd take for a long walk. We'd play with a ball in one of the off-lead areas in the compound to let off some steam, and then I'd snap on her lead, zip up my waterproof jacket and head out. We were lucky that the Old Windsor site was surrounded by rolling fields and beautiful walks along the Thames. The surrounding area was rural, with towpaths and meadows, plenty for dogs to sniff and see.

On one freezing cold day, we set off briskly out of the Battersea site, crossed the main road and went down the hill towards the river. Despite her strength, Foxy was lovely to walk. She never pulled you forward or tugged at her lead. We bounced along at a comfortable pace alongside the fields that stretched out to our left, and Foxy was enthralled by all the sights and smells. Usually, the fields were full of cows while the ditches were occupied by rabbits and other interesting little creatures.

Foxy was sniffing around as usual when suddenly she began investigating something seriously, pulling hard and trying to get under the barbed wire separating us from the dipped area that led into the field beyond. I resisted her for a while, thinking it was a dead rabbit or something else I'd rather not see. But when she continued tugging, I gave in and had a quick look.

What I saw made me gasp. There, in the ditch next to the barbed wire, was an emaciated dog.

She was so thin that I thought she must be dead. But then she moved her head. She was in the most appalling state and barely hanging on in the cold.

Foxy looked at me with eyes that said: *What's going on?*

I reached into my pocket to grab my phone and dial Battersea for more hands to help, when I remembered I'd left it charging back in the staff room. It was Murphy's Law. We had to keep our mobiles on us in case there was an emergency, and the one morning I really needed mine its battery had packed up as my shift had begun.

I knew that the dog needed immediate help, but I was worried she'd disappear if I went to fetch someone. There wasn't any other choice though so I sprinted back to the Home with Foxy and we burst into Reception. I was gasping but managed to explain what we'd found, hoping and praying the dog wasn't capable of running away because, if she disappeared, I was certain she'd die.

Her situation was upsetting but there was no time to dwell on that. I took Foxy back to her kennel and, with two other members of staff, headed out once more with blankets in hand to bring the dog in.

She was quite difficult to locate the second time, without Foxy's exceptional sense of smell, but in the end we found the ditch and climbed carefully over the barbed-wire fence.

The dog was still there, curled up in a ball. Although I'd been running around and was wearing thick layers, my cheeks and fingers ached from the cold and I could only imagine how frozen that dog was without an ounce of fat on her to keep her warm.

I stood by as the two members of staff carefully wrapped her in a blanket and lifted her up. She screamed in fear.

We returned to Battersea and took her straight to the clinic where a vet and a nurse were waiting. As we took a good look at the dog, we were all horrified. The vet, Paul, said: 'This is the worst state I've ever seen a dog in.'

Even for me, having spent years in Greece where that type of find was common, it was one of the most extreme cases of emaciation in a dog I'd ever seen. We reckoned she was a Great Dane and she should have weighed around forty kilos. On the scales, we saw she weighed just fifteen. 'How is she still alive?' I wondered.

'Your guess is as good as mine,' Paul said.

It was frightening even to touch her because she was like a skeleton and we worried we'd hurt her. We gave her some dog biscuits, which she gobbled, then stood her up to examine her – she had no wounds or cuts. When we saw she was able to hold herself up, we tried walking her the few steps to the kennel in the block adjacent to the clinic for sick dogs. She took three steps and collapsed. She was too weak even to lift her legs and get into the bed we'd set up for her in the kennel – the edge was only three inches high – so we got rid of it and padded an area with soft warm duvets instead.

She was filthy but we couldn't clean her up – she was too poorly for that – and as soon as we placed her on the duvets, she let out a big sigh and her eyes began to close. It was as if she knew she was finally safe.

As she settled in, the girls and I entered her details on to the database and set about picking a name for her. Around Christmas, it was quite normal for us to pick festive names but I said: 'Can we name her something that isn't so cheesy?'

We had a think and one of the girls said: 'What about Faith?'

It was perfect, given how much hope we needed even to dream that she would survive.

I returned home that night, drained. Instead of waiting a week to go in for my usual Tuesday shift, I found myself back at Battersea two days later. I checked in on Faith: she'd been cleaned up and was tentatively on her feet, her tan fur visible, along with her ribcage, but I was relieved to see her up and about.

I spoke to Paul, who told me Faith was at the start of a long road to recovery. He explained that when a dog is as malnourished as Faith, the sudden introduction of a normal amount of food could overload her system: to begin with, she was to be fed little and often. Even though she was hungry and demolished anything remotely edible that came her way, she would have small meals, specially prepared, throughout the day. The clinic had arranged a tailored feeding plan to get Faith, who was eleven or twelve months old, back to health without sending her system into shock.

Every week, I saw Faith improve. She had a sparkle

in her eyes and was proving to be a lovely, happy dog, in spite of her ordeal. It was amazing how quickly she was recovering emotionally from what she'd been through: she trusted the people around her at Battersea. Everybody loved her.

Her story had touched a lot of people, and I wasn't surprised when I heard a friend of the Home – an experienced Great Dane rescuer – had stepped in to adopt her.

But, as we headed into early December, there was a delay. Faith's new owner, Annie, had been rushed to hospital for emergency surgery. Faith was in need of special care and, although she was steadily gaining weight, she was still rather weak so I offered to foster her until Annie was better.

As is normal procedure, two of the foster co-ordinators from Battersea brought Faith to my home to check how she would interact with my dogs: Nelly, a Greek rescue, and Henry, a five-month-old Golden Retriever. Faith growled and lunged at them, and we were concerned that my home wasn't right for her. Then, as I studied her body language, I saw that Faith wasn't being aggressive, she was just an under-socialized dog.

I told the foster co-ordinators my plan and they agreed to leave Faith with me: I'd fostered many dogs in my time and was experienced at it.

I used a baby gate to separate Faith from Nelly and Henry so they could all see but not get at each other. Within a day, Faith had calmed down and I was able to let her mix with my dogs under supervision. She had no idea how to play with toys such as tennis balls, or even with other dogs, and was only interested in food.

Henry, though, as a young puppy, was determined to play with his new friend. He ran towards Faith, then ducked away at the last moment, gently yapping at her as if to say, *Come on!* until, eventually, she joined in. Thereafter they raced around the garden regularly, and the only time they weren't together was when Faith caught a whiff of one of my fruit trees and ran to the back of the garden to eat the windfall apples. She was still constantly foraging, and though she was gaining weight, it was a continuous reminder that she had been starving for a long time before we found her.

Two weeks passed and, early in December, Annie was ready for Faith. I took her back to Battersea and had a bit of a hard time letting her go. She was a special girl and I had a real soft spot for her because she'd been so ill. I knelt down and said: 'Good luck, Faith. Be a good girl. I love you.' Then I handed her over to a rehomer and walked away, as the tears stinging my eyes threatened to spill over.

When I glanced back, Faith was standing to attention and watching me with an expression that could only have meant: *Where are you going?*

That was what I found so hard about fostering. The dog doesn't know it's a temporary arrangement so it gets attached to you, as it would to its loving owner. My only comfort was that I knew where Faith was going: she would live a comfortable and happy life.

I returned to my regular Tuesdays, and Foxy was still waiting for our walks. In time, a man and his son fell in love with her and, though she was still wary of men, they were determined to give her a good life. They returned to the Home every day for weeks to spend hours with Foxy, taking her for walks and playing with her until she trusted them and was ready to go home.

It was lovely to see an owner so dedicated to Foxy and I knew she was in safe hands.

Months later when she returned to Battersea with her new owners for a spot of filming for Battersea, she recognized me from afar. Instead of looking at the camera, as she had been, she was now staring intently at me and wagging her tail. It was heart-warming that she remembered me, and it's moments like that and even the goodbyes, like the one with Faith, that make volunteering at Battersea so worthwhile.

From the Brink . . .

For as long as I could remember, our house was full of noise. My brother and I grew up on my parents' farm where we had land and livestock to tend, plus a small army of working dogs and family pets, like Springer Spaniels and Jack Russell Terriers. Life was busy and our house was packed. It wasn't unusual to find one of our lambs amid the dogs sleeping by the fire in the evenings. I adored our lifestyle, and when I was seven years old, I vowed to have dogs of my own when I grew up.

At nineteen, I moved into my own home and took in my first puppy, a Great Dane. In time, my family grew with twins, Joe and Betty, and later, when we moved to a twelve-acre smallholding, so did the number of pets. I was particularly fond of Great Danes, which I had learnt from experience were intelligent, sensitive and loved to relax. Later, I took in Maverick and Sky from a Great Dane rescue home, as well as two Terrier crosses, Kevin and Bertie, from Battersea Dogs & Cats Home.

I made some firm friends at Battersea and stayed in touch with some of the staff.

One evening, I was checking my emails when one in particular caught my eye. I clicked into it and found a picture that made me gasp. It was of an emaciated dog called Faith. She was a Great Dane cross and, judging from how she looked, she was lucky to be alive.

Below that shocking picture, there was a message from my friend at Battersea, explaining that Faith had been found close to death in a ditch near Battersea Old Windsor. It was likely somebody had dumped her there, knowing she could die in the bitter cold.

As I read the details, I felt desperately sorry for the dog.

At the end of the email, the sender asked: *Wouldn't Faith be happy with you???????*

I looked at my lovely dogs, snoozing beside the open fire in our cosy living room, all with full bellies, and I knew the answer. Yes, of course Faith would be happy with us. She thoroughly deserved a life like that of Bertie, Kevin, Maverick, Sky and Lola, a six-year-old rescued Great Dane. I typed back: *Yes! I'd love Faith to come and live with us.*

She'd come along at the right time. I'd been thinking of getting a playmate for Lola. While Bertie and Kevin were thick as thieves, and Maverick and Sky were older and happy to keep each other company, Lola was on her own. As a result, she'd lost her drive to play and run and was putting on weight. She'd actually become very lazy. If Battersea concluded that Faith was suitable for our household, she might turn out to be the perfect friend for her.

I knew from experience that Great Danes didn't cope well in the kennel environment so when a rehomer from Battersea called to discuss things in more detail, I told her: 'I can take Faith as soon as possible.'

'She's very underweight and is still under the care of our veterinary team, but she's getting stronger. As soon as she's well enough, hopefully in a week or so, we'll bring her to your home to see how she gets on with your other dogs and we can take it from there.'

'That sounds like a plan.'

Sometimes things don't go as you hope they will. The week Faith was due to visit, I became seriously ill and was in hospital for two weeks. I emailed Battersea and told them what had happened. They were very understanding: they would place Faith in foster care until I was well enough to have her.

In mid-November, I returned home and arranged with two rehomers at Battersea to bring Faith to my house in the countryside. It was unusual for my first meeting with Faith to be at my home, and for her to be introduced to the other members of my family on our territory, but since I'd been so ill, I was unable to make the four-hour drive to the Home, and on that occasion the rehomers made an exception.

Days later, when Faith was due to arrive, the dogs started barking all at once. That meant only one thing in our home: somebody was nearing our front door. I moved the bigger dogs to another part of the house and brought Bertie and Kevin into the living room.

The bell rang, and when I opened the door, two rehomers from Battersea stepped inside with Faith, who was still underweight but much better than she had been in the pictures I'd seen of her. It was immediately clear to me that she had some German Shepherd in her: she had the longer muzzle and a pointy nose, rather than the square, jowly look of my other Great Danes. She also had one ear up, the other down – adorable.

Faith was on a lead, and as Bertie and Kevin barked their curious hellos at her, she seemed bewildered. But Faith was as interested in them as they were in her. My dogs settled down beside me, and now that Faith was off the lead, she came over to me. She was friendly, if a bit nervous, but as I stroked her, she visibly relaxed and her ears flopped down. She wasn't on high alert any more. She pushed against my hand, begging to be stroked some more. Whenever I stopped or slowed, she nudged me.

'It must have been the German Shepherd strong will

that got her through that horrible time,' I told the ladies from Battersea. 'That's how she survived.'

They nodded.

I'd been kept in the loop on Faith's progress while she'd been at Battersea and was told she was now on four meals a day and steadily putting on weight. Nevertheless, her bones still jutted out, which was a stark reminder of the terrible condition she'd been found in.

'What monster could leave a dog in that state?' I wondered aloud.

There was no answer to that question so I continued: 'Well, it doesn't matter any more because, if she stays here, I will give her the life she deserves.'

I was handed a letter from Faith's foster carer, Helle, which detailed what she'd been feeding her. She added that Faith was food-driven and would eat anything we left out, so I should be careful about that.

Afterwards, the rehomers and I introduced Faith to Lola in an enclosed area outside. They hit it off immediately. They ran around after each other and it was nice to see them playing so well together. Through the fence, Faith caught a whiff of Sky and Maverick, and there weren't any problems there either.

It was clear to everyone that Faith was a good match for our home so I signed the relevant paperwork and the rehomers gave me a few days' supply of food for Faith and wished me all the best.

That night, I kept Lola and Faith together in the kitchen and the other dogs in another part of the house.

Faith slept well through the night and it seemed she was comforted by Lola's presence. Next day she had a proper introduction to the other dogs and was excited by all the company and attention. Every now and then, though, she became overwhelmed and came to find me, hovering with a look that pleaded: *Help!*

I'd give her a cuddle and then she'd be off again with her new friends.

Whenever Lola went outside, Faith followed her and they'd play for a while before Faith ran out of energy and came in. She didn't understand that her bed was hers alone and it was her special place to rest so she didn't get into it. When she did, she wouldn't stay in it for more than a few minutes. Joe, Betty and I took turns in the evening sitting beside her while she was in it, stroking her and giving her treats when she climbed in until, eventually, she'd grasped that it was hers.

Faith got on fine with Sky and Maverick, but Maverick suffered physical problems that left him uninterested in play. Lola was quick to show Faith the ropes, telling her: *No, steer clear of him!* The same went for Sky. I always joked she was an old dog in a young dog's body and she showed no interest in Faith. She was much more interested in keeping Maverick company.

As Christmas was round the corner, I bought a tree, put it up in our lounge and Betty helped me decorate it. On Christmas Day, we had lots of friends over and everyone got up early to take the dogs for a walk. When we returned, we cracked open the champagne extra early and celebrated. With Faith in the house, everybody seemed more excited than usual.

We sat down to lunch at two o'clock and afterwards opened our presents. The dogs had stockings filled with chews and were treated to slices of turkey. I'd never seen so many wagging tails! After that, the house quietened as I got a fire going and we settled in to watch a film. Maverick took his place by the open fire, Sky curled up on the sofa directly next to him, while Lola basked in the warmth nearby. Faith was happier in her own bed next to my chair, but Bertie and Kevin took turns on my lap. It was the same scene as when I'd first received the email from Battersea, except now I was no longer imagining Faith as a part of our family – she *was* a part of it.

In the New Year, I increased Faith's portion sizes and her weight gradually went up. Her ribs were no longer protruding, and her hip bones didn't jut out. She had bags of energy and couldn't sit still for long. Luckily, our smallholding was the perfect place for her. Our land was fenced in so the dogs had the run of it whenever they wanted and nosed around our horses and pigs.

Whenever Joe got the quad bike out, Lola loved to run after him. It was a favourite of the Great Danes in our household to chase after and outrun it. At first, Faith was terrified but Lola circled back and nudged her forward, then set off after Joe once more. It didn't take Faith long to catch on and join in.

Lola was five years older than Faith and, as I watched the two together, I developed a theory. I reckoned Faith had been weaned early from her mother and hadn't received a lot of attention from her, apart from being told off. She didn't understand that she had to observe the other dogs' boundaries and, as Helle had warned in her letter, had a habit of gobbling the others' food. Lola didn't let her get away with it. If Faith went for her food, Lola told her in no uncertain terms: *Hey, it's not OK to nick mine!*

In time, Faith learnt to behave and her confidence grew. She realized that if Lola went somewhere it was safe for her to go there too.

I worked from home so every morning I took the two of them for a long walk into the fields down the lane from our home and again in the evening. By now Faith was 20 kilos, up six from when she'd been found by Battersea but she was still underweight, which meant she felt the cold. On our walks in the winter air, she wore a special quilted coat to keep her warm.

Faith and Lola were together all the time and Faith took her cues from her friend. She learnt to play and run, and her energy rubbed off on Lola. She was no longer the lazy, snoozing dog I'd come to know. Instead of sticking beside me on long walks, she was chasing after Faith, who loved running ahead. Lola shed the extra weight she'd been carrying and was only in her bed when she was sleeping.

By spring, Faith no longer needed the coat and had blossomed into a lovely, bouncy, energetic dog. Last time we weighed her, she was forty-two kilos, which is just about where she should be. She's no longer the skeletal dog I first saw in that picture: she's muscular and healthy and does everything with passion. She has a real survivor's attitude and has moved onwards and upwards, not letting her sad past hold her back.

It is seeing her now, healthy, happy and with an amazing quality of life, that makes the rescue process so worthwhile. She's so loving and, of all my dogs, she's up there with Kevin as the rescue dog that has changed most.

He was young when we got him and he was quite the devil dog. He'd bite you as soon as you'd look at him because he was so scared and stressed out. Now he's the soppiest thing.

In my years rescuing Great Danes and terriers, I've realized that, no matter what their breed or history, all they need is time, routine and love. It's amazing how quickly a rescue dog, like the ones you find at Battersea, learns to trust you. Of course, there's always a bit of a concern when you're taking on a new dog that she or he will get on with the existing household, but experience has taught me to give them time to settle in.

If you are thinking about getting a dog, everything will be fine, as long as you have the time and patience to help the animal get into your routine. The work Battersea does is phenomenal and they need owners like you and me to help them keep doing what they do. It takes time and effort but it's worth it.

When Faith arrived, she hadn't had a chance to learn

the basics of living with a family or other dogs. She had had limited interaction and play with her mum and siblings but it was obvious that she wanted to be a good dog and simply didn't know how to go about it. Now she's got the picture. She's still got some growing up to do but she's getting more relaxed and secure in herself as time goes on. She is the sweetest dog.

Betty and Joe are animal mad and, like me, grew up in a house filled with them. They're nineteen now, but they learnt to walk by hanging on to one of our Great Danes, who would stand perfectly still until the twins had pulled themselves upright and taken a step forward.

Memories like that make up our family's history, and without our dogs, life simply wouldn't be the same. Faith was the missing member of our family and I didn't know it till she was here. Now we feel complete.

3. The Friendship of a Lifetime

I was strolling through Battersea Park in the late autumn, and as the leaves dropped to the ground, disturbed by probably the last warm breeze before the bitter gales of winter swept in, I felt a jumble of emotions course through me. Wherever I looked, couples and families were enjoying their outings, relaxed and carefree. Even the people I saw wandering around on their own had company in the form of their much-loved dogs.

But for me London had become a lonely place. I was thirty-five years old and coming out of the latest of what I could only describe as a string of failed relationships. I'd hit rock bottom. I took a seat on a bench and contemplated how I'd got there. I didn't have all the answers, but I knew some things for sure. I didn't have a job, I didn't have any money, and I didn't have anybody to love or to love me back. Where had it all gone so terribly wrong?

Just as these thoughts whirred around in my mind, a furry face appeared in front of me. The Springer Spaniel jumped around at my feet and stared at me eagerly. 'What are you looking for?' I said.

He disappeared under the bench and popped out a few seconds later with a tennis ball in his mouth. I expected him to run off now that he had what

47

he'd come for, but he wagged his tail and brushed up against me. For a moment, he stilled, resting his body against mine, and I stroked his head. It felt nice and I could tell he was enjoying it too: his breathing slowed and his head drooped. I felt my mind clear and, for a moment, peace.

Just then I heard a shout and the dog's ears twitched. It was clearly the voice of his master and, with a momentary glance at me, he was off. I watched them play together and thought how lovely it must be to have a dog to call your own, to love and be loved back unconditionally, without fuss or fanfare.

Weeks passed, and I couldn't get the idea out of my head. One day, I left my home and walked the short distance to the place I hoped would answer my prayers: Battersea Dogs & Cats Home. I walked slowly around the kennels and stopped at every one. *Are you the one I'm looking for?* I wondered, peering in. The expressions on the dogs' faces made me think that perhaps they were asking themselves the same question about me. But none of them spoke to me in the way I hoped my dog would.

That day, I didn't have any success and the same thing happened on my second visit.

But on the third, I got chatting to a rehomer, Sarah, and told her I was hoping to find a terrier, maybe a Jack Russell. I wanted a strong, spirited animal with a resilient character and reckoned a terrier would fit the bill nicely. I said: 'I saw three back there, could I meet them?' When I told her the names of the dogs I had in mind, she explained they needed more experienced owners, not a new one like me, to cope with their needs.

I felt a bit deflated, until she said: 'Mark, how do you feel about a puppy?'

My eyebrows must have shot up because Sarah led me to the puppy area and let me take in the activity before me. There were half a dozen puppies of different breeds and sizes running about. They instantly put a smile on my face. 'What a sight!' I laughed.

Sarah smiled back. 'What do you think?'

I scanned the kennels for a moment and that was when I spotted him. There, in the middle of an enclosure, was a St Bernard puppy, sitting bolt upright in his bed. But it wasn't him who had caught my eye. It was the tiny Jack Russell puppy latched on to the St Bernard's bed that had my attention. He was less than half the size of the other puppy but he was dragging the bed, with the St Bernard in it, across the floor.

I'd been hoping for a small dog with a big attitude so I pointed him out. 'That's the little man for me.'

I sat on the floor and called to the puppy, which bounded over to me. He was interested in every movement I made and every word I spoke to him. He nibbled at my hand, as puppies do, and licked my palm when I held it flat. We spent ten minutes playing and getting to know each other, and at the end of our session, I knew he was the one.

I had a chat with Sarah about my circumstances – the regular jobs I'd been doing as a gardener had dried up and I was currently unemployed, but that meant I had twenty-four hours a day to dedicate to a dog – and she agreed that the puppy, who was three months old, and I were a good fit. 'You can come and pick him up next week,' she said.

A rush of emotion went through me. For the longest time, I'd been looking at my life quite negatively, and here I was, deemed fit to look after a puppy. Suddenly I felt very proud. It was validating and made me believe in myself.

I walked outside into the winter sunshine and made myself a promise. Whatever was going on in my life, I'd keep my work van insured, taxed and on the road with a full tank of fuel. I knew if I achieved that, I'd strive to find gardening work, and when I managed that, I would always have money. Then, no matter what was going on, I could take my puppy out and about with me and for adventures in and around London.

Up until now, I hadn't coped well emotionally when things had gone wrong, but I could feel in my bones that my commitment to the puppy would do me a world of good.

Over the next week I cleaned and tidied my basement flat, which had a small yard, and bought my puppy – I'd decided to call him Jake – a bed, some bowls and everything else I thought he would need. 'I'm getting a puppy and I'm going to call him Jake,' I told my friends. I was so excited.

When I finally picked him up, I tucked him into the top of my jacket for the short walk home. It was

December and Jake hadn't had his second lot of shots so I made sure he was nice and toasty. When we arrived, he was soon sniffing everywhere and everything. It was all new to me, and I didn't have a clue what I was doing, so after Jake settled down, I set about reading the literature Battersea had given me, and thinking over their advice.

I knew they were at the end of the phone, ready to help if I needed them, but I told Jake: 'We'll figure this out as we go along, eh?'

I toilet-trained him – he caught on very quickly. He was a smart little boy and everything I had hoped for. As I was able to spend twenty-four hours a day with him, we soon formed a beautifully strong bond. He was so inquisitive and playful, and he had me thinking on my feet. I made up games to play with him, like hiding things and encouraging him to find them, or distracting him when he had a nibble of my boots or something else he wasn't supposed to get hold of. I was amazed at how intelligent he was, and wilful too. He had all the good qualities of a person, but lacked the complications that I'd grown to dislike: I loved Jake and he loved me back. I kept him company, and he was always as excited to see me as if he hadn't seen me for a month.

Every morning I was up at six thirty, and Jake bounced around until I was washed and dressed. Then we'd head out. I took Jake for walks around Battersea Park and realized, to my joy, that I was now one of those people with a lovely dog to call my own. It was nerve-racking at first because Jake was only tiny but he wanted to play with every dog he met. I soon got used to it – the other dogs were either friendly or just ignored him.

It took Jake six months to figure out that he wasn't going to catch a pigeon before it took off and he was never going to be as fast as the squirrel that taunted him every day. But he loved chasing them and I loved watching him.

When my gardening jobs picked up, we'd hop in the van together and Jake would join me in the driver's seat, curl up on my lap and snooze the journey away. While I worked, he would mill around, finding things to do. He'd sneak the empty plant pots I left to a quiet corner and pile them on top of each other, or he'd stare and yelp at any earthworms I'd dug up.

A one-hour job would take me two because he'd get under my feet and run along a newly prepped bit of soil. But it didn't matter: having Jake in my life had become all-consuming and I loved every minute of it. For so long, I'd been a perpetual worrier but now I had Jake I was doing things instead of worrying about them. Instead of wondering whether or not something was a good idea, I was busy taking care of the little being who depended on me for love, comfort, food and drink, and constantly demanded my attention.

Jake had given my life purpose. It was real and tangible and I couldn't quite get over the magical feeling that he was all mine.

On our car journeys he loved sticking his little face

out of the window and sometimes a leg too. I'd laugh at him. 'Come on, Jake, keep your elbows inside.'

He'd give me a look that said: *Yeah, what are you going to do about it, Dad?*

When Jake was a year old, we revisited the places in Surrey where I'd grown up, the woods I'd spent the summer holidays exploring with my friends, and the parks where I'd played football late into the evening. We stopped beside my favourite parts of the rivers and canals I'd known like the back of my hand. Now I was seeing things in a different light. With Jake, every day was a new adventure, a new experience. He was so excited by everything and loved racing around sniffing this and exploring that. I had to admit, it was rubbing off on me.

All the while, I was beginning to understand that, since my early teens, I'd been suffering with a depression that I could recognize only now, as it was lifting, for what it was. And I knew what was healing me from the inside out: Jake.

Having Jake to take care of was therapeutic. We went for walks and played together every day. We were, in a word, inseparable. Jake came with me when I saw my friends. He was great with people and was always a talking point. If I ever had to go out for a couple of hours without him, I'd leave Radio 4 on for him. I knew he'd be all right for toilet breaks because I'd taught him to use the cat flap to pop in and out.

After a couple of years, my life had taken a certain

shape. If Jake wasn't welcome at somebody's home, rather than go along with it, as I might have done in the past, I simply stopped socializing with that person. Jake did me a massive favour in making me stand up for him and, ultimately, for myself. And, with that, I focused on the things I wanted in life.

I worked hard and, two years later, bought a lovely little river boat for Jake and myself. We moved in and set up home beside the river in Chertsey, Surrey. Though Jake wasn't fond of the water, he loved everything around it. He hopped on and off when he needed a loo break, and if there was a patch of sunshine pouring into the boat, he was in it. He'd lie there until he was so hot he was panting, then slide into a shady patch until he'd cooled down, and repeat the whole cycle.

Our walks in Battersea Park were replaced with early-morning strolls along the foggy river, and the pigeons he loved to chase were replaced by ducks and geese.

In time, I built up the life Jake and I had together. I bought a better van and nipped into London to do my gardening rounds. For our time off, I bought an Ordnance Survey map of wherever we were moored and we'd go exploring.

Normally, Jake would wake up in the night at one or two o'clock and hop off the boat to have a wee. The tap, tap, tap of his paws usually woke me and I'd stay awake till he was back. But one night he didn't return in the normal few minutes. I stood up and opened the door – and that's when I heard the most almighty howling.

I dashed on to land and sprinted towards where the

sound was coming from. I got to him as he was dragging himself out of the bushes. My eyes stung with tears. Jake's back legs and tail were limp and he was howling with pain.

I picked him up, put him into the van, and rushed to the twenty-four-hour vet I'd registered him with. There, the junior vet gave him a shot of morphine and put him gently into a kennel. We'd have to wait until nine a.m. before they could operate. The vet didn't know what was wrong with him and I left in a panic.

I didn't sleep until the vet, Gerrard, called the next morning. 'I think he's burst a disc and is going to need emergency surgery.' There was a pause. 'He might not make it, Mark.'

I nodded silently into the phone, then said: 'Do what you can.'

'I'll call you later.'

Every minute was like an hour as I waited for news until, finally, I learnt that the operation to remove the ruptured disc had gone well. I was desperate to see Jake but Gerrard said it was best that he didn't move or get excited so I should wait for twenty-four hours.

The next morning, I was the first person at the surgery. I'd picked up a packet of ham, Jake's favourite treat, but when I saw him, he refused to look at me. I sat with him and softly reassured him that I wasn't going to leave him alone again. After thirty minutes, he turned to me, eyes blazing with emotion. *Don't. Do. That. To. Me. Again.*

Then he snapped the ham out of my hand.

'That's my boy,' I said.

Later, Gerrard told me the nerve in Jake's back had been severely pinched and he would need a lot of physio and care over the next year to get his legs functioning again. I told him I'd do whatever it took.

The following day I visited Jake in the clinic and carried him into its little garden. His back had been completely shaved and he had stitches running from his neck to his tail. He wasn't moving or excited by anything, so I hoped the fresh air would help. As we sat there, the birds were chirping and, suddenly, a squirrel dashed across the garden wall to the side of us. Jake's ears pricked up. He followed the squirrel with manic eyes and began to bark.

I knew then that, together, we'd do it.

I had three months off work and took Jake to hydrotherapy and physiotherapy every day. I learnt how to massage his legs to help build his strength until he was able to stand up, walk and, eventually, run. He couldn't jump any more but that didn't stop him. Life continued and many years passed.

Every Christmas, I got out his antlers and little cape and dressed him up. He loved Christmas as much as I did, and when I met someone special, Melanie, Jake loved her too. He was always so excited to see her whenever she visited and loved having her attention. He still dug for moles and had silly moments – even aged sixteen, he could throw you a dirty look like no human I'd ever known – but as he got older, he slowed down a bit.

One afternoon, I was fetching something from the

van and Jake was sniffing about by our favourite willow tree next to the river. The next time I looked up, he was gone. I had a sinking feeling in the pit of my stomach and my senses were on high alert. Something was terribly wrong. I rushed to the spot where I'd seen him last, then heard splashing and whining.

That was when I spotted Jake in the water. He hated it and was struggling to stay afloat. I reached in just as he plunged under the surface and pulled him out. His eyes had glazed over and I shouted at him to breathe as I rubbed his chest. Suddenly, he took a breath and coughed up a lot of water – I could see he'd had a real fright. I took him inside, dried him off and treated him to some chicken before placing him in his bed.

I sat beside him and thought: *That's put a real strain on his heart.*

When he started wriggling in pain, I took him to the vet, who gave him painkillers and offered antibiotics in case he'd swallowed anything nasty in that water. But the look on his face told me all I needed to know. The antibiotics would be useless because Jake wasn't going to recover. He said: 'Would you like to leave Jake here, with us?'

I shook my head. I took him home and held him in my arms. It was obvious that Jake was fading but he kept fighting it. Even in his last moments he was fighting it. So I held him close to me and whispered: 'It's OK to go now, Jake.' He slipped away in my hands.

Jake died on 14 December 2013. I'd had him for sixteen years and two days.

We buried him under his favourite willow tree and I kept a candle burning for him day and night. I even woke up in the early hours to light a new one. Even then, I half expected to hear the pitter-patter of his feet as he hopped outside for a wee.

Everything looked the same – the boat, the sky, the road, our things – but without Jake, everything felt different. My life had been structured around him for so long that now the gaping holes in it were glaringly obvious and unbearably painful.

Christmas passed in a blur and Jake's presents sat wrapped up in the corner. He usually loved to rip off the paper and get to the good stuff he knew was waiting for him underneath.

Mel struggled, too, and we really felt Jake's absence.

I'd always vowed not to get another dog straight away, if something happened to Jake, but now I couldn't see another way around it – I couldn't stand being without my dog.

Before the New Year, Mel and I were talking and I told her: 'I think I'd like to get another dog.'

She nodded and said: 'It's quiet without him, isn't it?' A few days later, she said: 'Do you want to go to Battersea today?'

It was like one of those comedy moments in a cartoon when a light-bulb appears above a character's head. 'That's a brilliant idea,' I said. I knew that I'd like another puppy and I reckoned there would be a waiting list. 'Let's go and put our names down.' I was sure it would be a few months before we were lucky enough to get a puppy.

We went along to Battersea Old Windsor, near where we were moored up, and spoke to a rehomer there. As I told Ali about Jake and what I was hoping to find, a funny look crossed her face. 'It's strange you're saying this because we've just had a male Jack Russell cross puppy in. He arrived yesterday.'

I didn't know what to say so I waited for her to continue.

'Do you want to see a picture?' Ali said. She pulled up an image on her phone.

I laughed. 'Gosh,' I said, taking in the puppy's black coat, his tan face and paws. 'He's just like Jake.'

Ali told me Sprout was the last of a litter of six and his mother had started snapping at him. 'His owner was worried there was something wrong with him and his mum was rejecting him so she brought him in.'

'What happened?' I asked.

'We checked him over and assessed him thoroughly, but as we did that, we realized there's nothing wrong with Sprout – he's just a pest!'

I thought: *I like him already.*

'Would you like to meet him?

Mel and I went along to the puppy area and one of the other girls brought out the little Jack Russell cross. We had a play with him and I felt a jumble of emotions. I hadn't planned to leave with a dog but Sprout was so cute. On the other hand, I wasn't sure I was ready.

Ali came back and I smiled at her. 'What's happening?' I said.

'Do you want to take him?'

'So we can have him?' I replied, genuinely surprised that twice in a lifetime I'd been lucky enough to be deemed worthy by Battersea.

'You can have him tomorrow.'

Mel and I stepped aside and had a chat, then returned to the rehomer. 'Can I say yes, but ask you to let me sleep on it till tomorrow?' I said.

'Of course.'

I'd always joked that I was 'Never Ready Mark' so to make such a decision about the puppy was hard. I was completely torn because I was still grieving over Jake, but now I'd held Sprout in my arms, I didn't want anyone else to have him. 'Don't give him to anyone else, will you?' I said, just before we left.

Next morning, I woke up at six thirty, as always. I stared over to where Jake would normally have been snoozing and my heart felt heavy. But the confusion had lifted.

Mel and I returned to Battersea, ready to take our new dog home.

Milo, as we named him, literally pinged around the living area on the boat, jamming himself into every corner, sniffing this and sniffing that. He trampled over me in bed, knocked things over and pulled at the toilet paper. He was three months old and a complete scoundrel, just like Jake had been.

He had so much energy and personality – I'd forgotten what it was like to have a puppy around. It was a fabulous distraction but only for minutes at a time. I kept calling him Jake by accident, and when I took him to the vet two weeks later to register him, I made a confession: 'I'm so close to taking him back to Battersea, Gerrard. I just can't help how much I miss Jake. And Milo isn't Jake.'

Gerrard was sympathetic. 'It takes a bit of time. You owe yourself that, and you owe Milo that.'

I could see where he was coming from and I returned home with a new take on things. I'd made a commitment to Milo and I wasn't about to quit. Instead of focusing on Jake's absence, I focused on Milo more closely. I tried to get to know him. We played together, and whenever the sun spilt in through the window, I noticed Milo lay there until he was so hot he was panting, just like Jake had. It was a comfort.

Slowly, his personality started to shine through, and once he was able to go outside and we went on walks together, the bond really began to form. I realized how much I'd missed that routine and exercise. Everything always seemed better after a good walk.

Milo loved them too and he loved being around other dogs. He didn't care if it was a Chihuahua or a Dobermann – if there was another dog nearby he'd try his luck and ask if they wanted to play. He was fearless, so full of himself, and I loved that about him.

At home, he wanted our attention, and if we didn't give it to him, he'd throw his bed around. He'd gone through three by the summer. By then, I'd learnt that Milo loves water with the same passion that Jake had hated it. He came to work with me, and when I watered the garden, Milo stood at the end of the stream and snapped his jaws at the water, trying to catch it. He jumped in the river and loved to swim. He was a whirlwind.

At night, when he'd run out of steam and stopped trying to find the one item in the boat you'd chase him for, he'd settle between Mel and me on the sofa for a nap. Then I'd look at him, his tongue lolling out as he nestled his head on my lap, and feel fit to burst with love for him.

He's a cheeky little fella and he can be a pain in the bum sometimes, but he's *my* pain in the bum.

The last year has not been easy with the grief I felt for Jake . . . but then Milo came along. He's a big step forward in my life. He's made things complicated and pushed me into uncharted territory because he's Mel's dog as well as mine, but that's a good thing because we're moving forward.

Milo is not the dog I had before, and sometimes I feel guilty that I have a new dog, but life goes on, doesn't it?

There's no guarantee that I've got Milo for longer than another day, and that in itself has made me understand how very precious he is to me. In fact, he's just as precious as Jake was. He's already given me so much – I can't wait for Christmas, to pull out those antlers and sling that cape around his neck, because I know Christmas is going to be a blast this year with Milo around.

4. Brother from Another Mother

I was coming home from work when the London riots broke out in the summer of 2011. At first, it felt like a horrible nightmare. Then something happened that brought it much closer to home.

My partner Josh's sister Rosemary became a victim of the violence when her flat was burnt down. Luckily, she hadn't been there when it happened but firefighters had gone in to rescue her little cats, Pickle and Pootle, who were trapped inside.

They were both at death's door by the time the team reached them, brought back to life by the quick-thinking emergency services on the street.

Josh's sister and her two smoky cats came to stay with us. That much I was expecting, but what I wasn't expecting was how traumatized the cats would be. They were scared and jumpy and I felt desperately sorry for them.

As a child, I'd only ever briefly owned a dog and never had much of a connection with cats. But in the month that Pickle and Pootle were with us, I formed a deep bond with them. I found myself rushing home to see them every night, and when they left after a few weeks, I missed them. I missed their little faces and the unwavering love and affection they showed me whenever they were near. It had been a very special privilege to watch them recover from the fire, to go from crying, scared cats to boisterous and mischievous adventurers once more. I was honoured it had happened in our home. But, more than that, it was amazing how quickly the pair had felt like a part of the family, a part of our home, and I was sad when they left.

Josh and I decided to visit Battersea Dogs & Cats Home and put our names down for a kitten. We explained we were going on holiday, and were told that when we returned, we'd be in a good position to take one or two cats home.

I hadn't been sure about taking two but, months earlier, Josh and I had begun to talk in earnest about having a cat, or cats, while we had been on holiday in America. One afternoon we were driving from Phoenix to Tombstone, a town famous for its cowboy past, when Josh had said, 'We've just exchanged on our family home and, once it's renovated, we'll be in the perfect position to finally get a cat ... or two.' As our Jeep bounced along the highway, we talked about all our options, where we would get the cat from, where we would put its bed and even what we could name it. As we did, I flipped the radio station and a song blared out. It was a Jennifer Lopez number, featuring the rapper Pitbull, and when I heard the rap at the beginning, I laughed. 'Did you catch that?' I said. 'The lyric there?'

'Which bit?' Josh said.

'Something about Tonka. Isn't that a great name for a cat?'

'It *is* a great name,' he said. 'We need to keep Tonka on our radar.'

Next day, as we headed to New Mexico, we passed through a beautiful little Bohemian-looking town. It was filled with art galleries and we spent a blissful day there pottering about. At dusk we were driving out when we spotted a big sign at the side of the road: *You are now leaving Bisbee.* Josh said: 'Bisbee. That's a cool name for a cat.'

It was settled. Tonka and Bisbee were firmly on our list of favourite cat names and we agreed we would check out Battersea for cats to adopt.

We returned home from our holiday, renovated our house in south-west London and, more than a year after Pickle and Pootle had stayed with us, we started looking at the Battersea website.

One Sunday the profile of a beautiful silver tabby called Thunder caught my eye. When I showed Josh, he said: 'Let's go down next weekend.'

It seemed so far away when I wanted that cat there and then but, after a slow week at work, Saturday eventually arrived. We took ourselves off to Battersea. At Reception, our details were taken and we were interviewed. I was pleasantly surprised by how vigorous the interview process was. The lady asked all sorts of questions.

How long have you lived at your current home? Is it near a main road? Is there a cat flap, a garden, any other pets?

The questions went on and on. It was clear that Battersea were committed to making sure they matched potential owners with the right animal. Not only was an animal rehomed quickly, but it went to the right home.

Then she said: 'Finally, can I have a copy of your IDs and a recent utility bill?'

We handed them over. 'It's very thorough, this process, isn't it?' I said.

She smiled. 'It has to be, for the sake of both you and the animals.' Then she added: 'Just so you know, Battersea reserves the right to inspect the house and your living arrangements.'

We nodded.

Afterwards, we waited in the reception area for another member of staff to give us a tour of the cattery when I spotted a familiar face. He had silver fur and eyes that shone . . . It was Thunder and he was in a cat carrier being taken home by his new owners! I nudged Josh and the despair I felt was reflected on his face. Just like that, the gorgeous cat we'd set our hearts on was gone.

I felt deflated as I watched the couple disappear up the slope and out of the Home. Worse, when we got upstairs to the cattery, a lot of the pods were empty. Neither of us had had any idea how busy Saturdays were for Battersea and how many animals were rehomed at the weekend. I later discovered that over one bank holiday weekend alone thirty-six cats were rehomed.

It was now four thirty and, although a lot of pods were empty, there were still some animals waiting for new homes. Each one had a little description sheet stuck to the front. Some said the cat needed company, others that the owners needed previous cat experience, or that the cat couldn't be left alone during the day. A sinking feeling settled inside me. Perhaps we weren't meant to take home a cat today. Then I noticed one glass door with no information on it. Inside, a tabby cat was sitting on his haunches – and winking at us. I did a double-take. He really was winking at us. I nudged Josh. 'Look at that,' I said. 'Are you seeing this?'

'Yes, Niall, I see it.'

The cat really was blinking one eye at us. I went off to find a cattery assistant and asked her to help us. She followed me to the winking cat's pod and I said: 'What's the story with this cat?'

We learnt he was called Sammy: he was fine to be left alone, and no previous cat experience was necessary. 'He's only just come in but he's in great shape and ready to be rehomed. Would you like to meet him?'

My heart skipped a beat.

Was Sammy the one for us?

Josh, or Dr Doolittle, as I jokingly called him, and I were allowed inside the pod for a bit of socializing with Sammy. He was very calm and friendly, and as we crouched down to stroke him, he brushed his tail against us. He wasn't hissing or frightened, but totally at ease. Of course, within seconds he was all over Josh and purring away. I had had no experience with cats but, from what I could see, Sammy was a beautiful friendly cat and I was really taken with him, as was Josh.

67

We were in there for five minutes and we'd made our choice. When the Battersea rehomer returned, Josh and I found ourselves saying in unison: 'We'll take him.'

She gave us a confused look. 'You'll take both?'

'What do you mean, both?' I asked.

She pointed behind us to a cardboard box. I lifted the flap across the top and inside was a ginger tom. He was shaking uncontrollably. The poor sausage was scared out of his mind. It threw me but Josh's eyes lit up. I knew what he was thinking. That two handsome little cats would be perfect.

As we popped the lid back down and gave the shaking cat some space, we learnt the two had been acquired from different litters but kept together by their owner in a fourth-floor flat.

Some people don't leave much information about the animal they have brought to Battersea, but Sammy and Tommy had been left with reams and reams. Our rehomer explained: 'It's quite unusual for us to have all this history but the lady who brought them in had written copious notes about what they liked, didn't like, their medical history and even their personalities.'

As she went to fetch the lady's notes, I felt really quite sad. It was obvious the cats' owner had loved them and to hear that she'd had to give them up for financial reasons was heart-breaking. The rehomer flicked through a thick binder that contained the notes and read out the bits she felt were important for us to know, starting with the medical stuff. Tommy had suffered a mouth problem so she fetched a vet to talk to us.

He examined Tommy's mouth and showed us his teeth and gums. 'He's in really good shape now,' he said, 'so there's nothing to worry about in terms of his previous problems.'

It was good to hear that. The vet continued to talk about both cats. 'They've had a battery of tests and are both healthy.' He told us that a lot of felines have a form of HIV, known as FIV, but that these two were in the clear. He stuck around to answer all our questions, even though it was well past closing time. He didn't rush us and was very patient. We truly felt we were in good hands. When he had said goodbye and left us, the rehomer told us more about the cats from the notes in the binder.

We learnt Sammy and Tommy's exact birthdays and more about their past. Though they were from different mothers, they had been taken in by their previous owner at the same time. 'They've never spent a day apart,' the rehomer said, 'and that is one of the strict instructions we were given by their owner. Under no circumstances should they be rehomed separately. They have to stay together.'

Josh's eyes were round with urgency – the urgency to say yes now. But I needed time to consider things. I'd gone from wanting a dog to wanting a cat, and now I was being offered two. 'Is it possible to have a think about it overnight?' I asked.

'Yes, of course. We'll reserve them for you but please let us know by tomorrow lunchtime as we really would like to rehome this pair quickly because, as you can see, Tommy is having a really tough time in here.'

I totally understood. But with the night to think about it, I was confident we would make the right choice, not only for the cats but for Josh and me, too.

Over dinner and late into the night, Josh and I talked about what it meant for us to have two cats instead of one. It was a bonus knowing the cats were happy to stay in all day and be alone while we were at work, and that they would keep each other company.

That night, I tossed and turned, replaying our visit to Battersea in my mind. In the morning, I woke to find a familiar face staring intently at me.

'So,' Josh said, 'have you decided?'

He'd obviously been awake for a while and, as the fog of sleep lifted from me, he didn't let up. He'd clearly been dying to find out what I thought. And he knew me better than anyone: I was a procrastinator and sometimes I needed a nudge to get into gear. It was lucky that he knew exactly how to press my buttons.

Josh said: 'Think of it this way, Niall. What if we say no and those beautiful cats end up in an abusive home?'

Well, that did it.

'As soon as they're open, we'll call Battersea and let them know we'll have them both.'

We made the call and headed straight to our local pet shop to stock up on everything we needed for Sammy and Tommy. Two days later, we returned to Battersea. Before we were given our cats, we were handed a rehoming pack and also some sound advice. 'As these two have always been indoors, leave it a significant amount of time before you let them out. That way they're unlikely to go out and never come back.'

I hadn't even thought of that.

'Try letting them out after two or three months. Also, try to keep them in one room for a week before letting them explore the rest of the house.'

I said: 'That's interesting. Why?'

'They've had a bit of trauma, first of all being uprooted from their home and owner, then coming to Battersea where it's noisy and busy and very different from what they're used to. Now, coming to your home, it will make them feel better to have one safe, secure and calm room to get used to before they venture further.'

It made perfect sense.

'Just make sure they have plenty of toys and access to litter trays,' the rehomer said, 'and visit their room to get to know them over that week.'

Finally, we were given the rehoming pack, then Sammy and Tommy were handed over to us.

Back home, we put down the cats' carry cases in a quiet, sparsely furnished room, and opened them. I was so excited to have them home that I pulled out my phone and began videoing their arrival.

Straight away, two very different and interesting personalities emerged.

Bisbee, as we'd renamed Sammy, was quite cocky in his approach. He strutted around the room and explored everything in his path. He sniffed and pounced and played in his new environment, brushing past us as he sashayed around.

Tonka, as we'd renamed Tommy, was the complete opposite. When he eventually came out of his box, he ran towards the curtain and hid behind it. He was so painfully shy that when I pulled the curtain back he looked away. It was endearing and heart-breaking all in one go.

That night, we retreated to the lounge and read the rehoming pack from cover to cover. It was written in a very straightforward and helpful way, explaining how to get Bisbee and Tonka used to their litter tray, how to begin getting them used to going outside, and why neutering cats is so important. When we had finished, we flicked back to the beginning and read it again to make sure we hadn't missed anything.

Over the next week, we could see Tonka was having a hard time and it was clear he was still quite traumatized. He couldn't bear to be looked at and spent most of his waking hours hiding. When he wasn't hiding, he was shaking.

We took Battersea's advice and gradually introduced the pair to more of the house. Tonka wouldn't often leave the room but Bisbee had a good snoop around.

After a week, we noticed Tonka's microchip was sticking out of his skin so I called Battersea, and was asked to take him in. It was a hard task getting him into his carrier, and once I'd managed it, Bisbee paced around me manically. It was difficult to see their distress at being separated but I knew it had to be done.

At Battersea, a vet checked Tonka over, quickly removed the chip and reinserted it. He gave Tonka a rub. 'It happens in a few cases but it should be OK now.' As easily as that, the problem was fixed and the boys were reunited. Bisbee had waited by the door till we returned.

Several weeks passed and, while Bisbee settled in, Tonka didn't want to interact with us and still hid all the time. Even though I'd witnessed Pickle and Pootle's trauma, and their gradual recovery, I was anxious about Tonka. What if he was an antisocial, unhinged cat? Josh reassured me and told me repeatedly to give him more time. I vowed to be more patient with him.

One night I was crashed out on the sofa after a particularly hard day at work when I felt something licking my toe.

I realized it was Tonka. He had left the cats' room and ventured into the lounge. Now he jumped up on to the sofa, tiptoed up beside me and took a seat right there on my stomach. Following weeks of us feeding him, being there for him and giving him what he needed, he had decided we were all right. I tried not to make any sudden moves and scare him off, just held my position, sprawled on the sofa, even though I wanted to squeeze him.

Instead I picked up the phone and called Josh, who was away on business, and told him about the breakthrough. He was as excited as I was so I took lots of pictures of Tonka napping on me and sent them to him.

From then on, it was as if a switch had been flicked. Tonka no longer hid behind the curtains and began to explore the house with fervour. He was finally home,

73

and we could get to know him properly. I learnt he was chatty and affectionate, as well as demanding. He wanted our attention, our cuddles and our cooing over him. But he was equally giving of his time and love.

Whenever either of us came home, Tonka was waiting at the door. To follow his miaows of 'Thank God you're home,' there were vigorous head bumps and demands for strokes . . . and food.

We learnt that if we were to put ten bowls of food in front of him, Tonka would not stop when he was full. Instead, he would methodically work through each one. We kept a keen eye on Bisbee's food in case Tonka made a beeline for it, which, if we weren't careful, he most definitely would.

Even when he didn't want more food, Tonka rushed up our clothes, climbing us until he reached a shoulder, then perched on it like a pirate's parrot to be as close to us, and any interesting action in the kitchen, as he could get. He was proving to be a right character and loved being around us.

At night, it became impossible to shut our bedroom door because he would sit outside and miaow until we gave in. Once that door was open, he jumped on to the bed and chatted away or kneaded our arms and backs, oblivious to the fact that we were trying to sleep.

If Josh and I ignored Tonka's vocalizations, it was only a matter of time before he started head bumping. After that he used his paw to tap us on the cheek. If we slept through that, the final stage was a gentle nip on the nostril. Josh complained about it every day but, deep down, he loved it.

Tonka monopolized Josh and often ended up sleeping on his pillow, snuggled under the duvet or sprawled out on him.

But it wasn't just us who enjoyed having an attention-seeking toddler in the house. Our parents were equally enamoured of Tonka and Bisbee. (Later, whenever we went away for work or a holiday, there was a scrap over who would cat-sit. It was on one such cat-sitting weekend that Tonka figured out a new skill: if he threw himself at the door handle with sufficient force, the door would open. At 5.5 kilos, he had enough strength to do it easily.)

One night, my parents came to stay after a trip to America, where their hotels had had twin beds. Before she retired upstairs, Mum joked: 'It's been great having my own bed. Tonight will be a bit of a challenge getting used to your father again!'

Off they went. Next morning, I asked how she'd slept.

A bemused look crossed her face. 'I woke up in the middle of the night,' she began, 'with your father snoring right in my face. I turned the light on to tell him off but it wasn't him. It was Tonka asleep on my pillow!'

I couldn't stop laughing. 'Poor Dad! He gets the blame for everything.'

Tonka's night-time adventures continued. Bisbee, on the other hand, liked nothing more than to relax with

Josh and me in front of the telly, or to sit quietly by himself in deep contemplation.

Being inside didn't stop Tonka getting up to mischief. Over a weekend, when we'd gone to Lisbon and a friend was popping in to check on the cats and feed them, Tonka went missing. We almost flew home when we found out but the flights were so expensive we had to rethink our strategy.

We knew all the windows and doors were locked so there was no chance he'd made an escape. He was probably snoozing in a cosy hiding place somewhere in the house. It was the only explanation.

But when we arrived back home, there was still no sign of him. Bisbee was sitting by the American-style fridge-freezer so we gave him some food and continued looking for Tonka.

In another room, I could hear Josh calling Tonka. He was becoming more and more distressed. He came back to the kitchen, tears streaming down his face. 'I think Tonka's gone up the chimney. He could be anywhere.'

As the more logical of the two of us, I told him to take some deep breaths. 'Let's just think this through,' I said.

Bisbee, though he'd been fed, was still staring at the fridge-freezer.

As I followed his gaze, I noticed something. There was a small 15-by-20-centimetre gap to the side of the unit. *Surely not . . .*

I climbed on to the counter and shone a torch into

the gap. And there, in the spotlight, two pitiful eyes were staring back at me.

It was Tonka! Somehow he'd fallen into the gap and got himself wedged halfway down between the fridge-freezer and the wall. I called for Josh who came running in. We ended up pulling the doors off the fridge-freezer to get him out.

As soon as we did, Tonka dashed to the litter tray. The poor mite hadn't made any mess while he'd been stuck.

It was a wonder he hadn't made any noise with all the calling we'd done for him. He was usually such a loud and talkative cat but we reckoned the fright of getting stuck had sent him into shut-down mode. After he'd had some food and water, though, he couldn't wait to tell us all about it. He climbed all over us, miaowing and chatting, cuddling into our arms while he talked and squeaked at us.

That was one life out of nine gone, for sure.

In mid-December, three months after the cats had come to live with us, I climbed into the loft and pulled down a number of specially labelled boxes. Each was marked 'CHRISTMAS' and was packed to the brim with baubles, tinsel, lights and other festive delights. Of course, for Tonka and Bisbee, it really was like all their Christmases had come at once. Every box had to be thoroughly investigated, and both trees, a real one for our downstairs living area and a fake one for our lounge upstairs, where we spent most of our time, were of great interest.

They bounced around as I tried to put up the decorations – it turned into a real mission, taking several hours longer than ever before. Everything that jingled was a target for pawing practice and, like two lithe little boxers, Tonka and Bisbee each picked one of the reflective disco-light-style baubles and went crazy for it.

Eventually, the trees were decorated and, for the most part, we kept the cats away from the real one in case they hurt themselves on the sharp pine needles. But the fake one upstairs became their new home – like a big climbing frame for cats. Bisbee was smaller so, with delicacy and agility, he climbed up into the tree and found a spot to settle near the warmth of the fairy lights. He napped his way through most of December in that tree.

Tonka, not one to be left out of anything fun, did the same. Only he knocked half of the decorations out of the tree as he climbed, making it sway from side to side before he settled opposite Bisbee. Every morning, I had to reconstruct Tonka's side of the tree and there were more than a few bauble fatalities.

One decoration stayed out of reach: the boys' stockings. I had bought four and stuck initials on: T, B, J, N. Josh and I filled Tonka and Bisbee's with cat-nip toys, little stuffed mice and treats and hung them high above the fireplace, ready for Christmas Day.

That first Christmas with Tonka and Bisbee was magical. Josh and I were finally in our dream home, a five-storey townhouse that we'd made our own, and now our family had expanded to four.

When my parents arrived, the Christmas presents under the tree quickly piled up –Tonka and Bisbee had more gifts than the rest of us combined. They were due to get thoroughly spoilt but we couldn't help ourselves.

On Christmas Eve, the house was full of family, hustle and bustle. During the day, Dad spent hours playing with Tonka, who loved chasing tennis balls, and Bisbee, who never tired of chasing a toy mouse on a string. In the evening, when we all settled in the lounge, the cats mooched from one person to the next, gaining cuddles and spoils as they went.

Next day, as Christmas got under way, Josh headed to the kitchen to cook up a storm while my mum got to know the cats a bit better. Ironically, she had always said she wasn't keen on animals, but whenever there was a pet about, it loved her.

By the time lunch was ready, my parents were smitten with the pair of them. And who wouldn't be? They were so handsome and so loving. It was impossible not to fall for them. Tonka and Bisbee were very much the stars of our Christmas and explored everything from wrapping paper to the presents under the tree. The first time Mum saw them climbing into the tree for a nap, she howled with laughter.

Meanwhile, it was a major task keeping them away from Josh who was cooking. They jumped up on to the counters despite our best efforts to keep them off, and we couldn't leave a single scrap of food out. To keep them occupied, we gave the boys their presents and they sprang into life. Tonka rolled around in feline heaven with his cat-nip toy and Bisbee adored his stuffed mouse. Like a dog, he padded around the house with it hanging out of his mouth. He hid it, found it, dragged it and squashed it all through Christmas Day. And at the end, the two dragged their favourite toys into the Christmas tree, found their respective spots halfway up and began to snooze. It was the funniest sight I'd ever seen. Before I knew it, I'd taken more than a hundred photos of our first Christmas together.

At work in the New Year, my desktop became more and more cat-oriented with pictures of Tonka and Bisbee on my computer and on my phone. I was becoming a crazy cat person, but I didn't care. Neither did Josh, though he did like to point out something every now and then: 'And you were the one who wanted a dog!'

It was true. But now we had Tonka and Bisbee, I couldn't imagine our lives without them.

Come Easter, I'd made every excuse to put off the final hurdle: letting them outside.

We'd installed a magnetic cat flap in the patio doors and Josh told me: 'It's time for Tonka and Bisbee to go outside.'

I was nervous, but I knew he was right.

It took Bisbee two days to figure out how the cat flap worked, but it was two weeks before Tonka had conquered it.

But conquer it they both did. They loved being outdoors and it was a real joy to watch them. Tonka and Bisbee explored every inch of the garden and quickly worked out they had an enemy lurking in the tree. Cyril the squirrel, as we called him, had made himself at home in our ash tree and the cats made it their life's mission to catch him.

Some time later, we had friends over for dinner and one was in the bathroom on the top floor when she let out a shout: 'Josh, Niall, you need to see this!'

I found her peering out of the window. I took her place, and when I looked out, I came eye to eye with Tonka, who was thirty feet up in the tree. He'd clearly been chasing Cyril and now he was stuck. It was worrying and, beside me, Josh was freaking out, as usual. I reckoned the safest thing to do was leave Tonka to his own devices and let him come down in his own time.

We didn't have to wait long. By the time we'd all gone into the garden with a box of his favourite treats to rattle, Tonka had embarked on a somewhat uncontrolled and rapid descent to the ground.

Josh let out a gasp beside me and rushed over to our cat, who had landed gracefully on his feet. 'You silly beast!' he said, scooping Tonka into his arms. 'What were you doing up there?'

Tonka turned casually to look at Josh, then me. There was a flutter of movement above us. There, high in the tree, was the squirrel. Tonka gave him a good stare and let out a miaow, but before he could jump out of Josh's arms for round two, Josh rushed inside. 'I'm not letting that happen again anytime soon.'

We set Tonka down and he waltzed off to his bed, oblivious to the drama that seemed to follow him everywhere he went.

In time, it became clear that Cyril wasn't the cats' only enemy knocking about the area. Next door, our neighbours had a yappy little dog that was constantly in and out of their back garden. Whenever they arrived home, the dog would start yapping. After a while, that kind of a noise becomes part of the background so it didn't bother us too much.

But one evening the dog was noticeably quiet. I pointed it out to Josh. 'Isn't that weird?'

'It is,' he replied, 'but at least we can have some peace now!'

Not ten minutes had passed when there was a knock at the door. Our neighbours were there, and they looked a bit pale. 'What's the matter?' I said. 'Is everything OK?'

'I'm not sure,' came the reply. 'Can you come next door for a minute?'

Down our steps we went, through the gate and up to the front door at our neighbours' home. It was open and we were ushered inside.

At first, I didn't spot anything out of place. Then, my eyes moved towards the stairs. At the top their little dog was sitting bolt upright and looking more than a little confused.

I nudged Josh and, as he followed my gaze, I tried desperately not to laugh because on either side of the poor little dog a cat was flanking him. One familiar grey one and the other his ginger brother. Tonka and Bisbee had snuck into the house and were now casually asleep beside the dog.

I turned to our neighbours with a sheepish grin. 'All

that breaking in must have knackered them out. Erm, so sorry about this . . .'

It hadn't been the first time they'd asked me to remove Tonka and Bisbee from their home as they often liked to sneak in.

I moved quietly up the stairs and scooped both of them into my arms. After that, the neighbours fixed their back door with a magnetic flap through which only their dog could pass.

Tonka and Bisbee's shenanigans with the locals didn't end there. When they were out in the garden, their favourite spot was on the fence to the left of the house. They'd often perch there, face to face, while keeping a watchful eye on their surroundings. Not much frightened Tonka but the neighbours to the left of us had an obese ginger female cat called Boo and she terrified him. Whenever he saw her, he'd slip into stealth mode, and would inch in super-slow motion towards the house, thinking that if he moved slowly enough, she wouldn't see him. Around Boo, Tonka was a complete coward.

But Bisbee was nothing of the sort. Whenever Tonka was in trouble or there was the slightest whiff of danger, Bisbee shot outside to protect his brother. His tail would fan out to five times its normal size and he'd instantly be ready for battle. It really was a sight to behold. One afternoon, Bisbee flew past me and out of the cat flap. All I could hear was a scuffle and a skirmish, then lots of hissing.

I looked out of the window and a panther-like black cat was trying to tear into Tonka. Before I could react,

Bisbee had jumped in and chased away the assailant. I felt like a proud dad as the two brothers limped back to the cat flap and sloped inside for a rest.

When each of their birthdays rolled round, Josh and I gave them a card signed by both of us and the other cat, plus special treats. Bisbee's favourite was prawns and Tonka's was chicken breast. We figured that out because whenever Josh or I had a prawn or chicken dish for dinner a little paw would creep in under an arm and try to snatch a bit.

That wasn't the only mischief Tonka got up to with his paws. When I worked from home, he milled about near me and sometimes jumped on to my desk. He'd watch my fingers tapping away on the laptop and suddenly pounce on them. Once, I untangled myself, looked at the screen and realized that everything was now in Chinese. In hitting some crazy cat combination on the keyboard, he had changed the language on my computer.

An awkward conversation ensued with the IT team at work, who had to fix the laptop. I couldn't bring myself to confess that my crazy cat had caused the problem.

When Christmas came round again, the minute those decorations were brought down from the loft, Bisbee and Tonka were straight in there. They sniffed at everything, pawed at every bauble and, once again, scrambled up the tree to have a nap. My life over the Christmas holidays seemed to revolve around scooping up the trinkets Tonka had knocked off the tree and putting them back in their place.

But it doesn't matter how much havoc they wreak on our lives, be it at Christmas, Easter, the weekend or just another week night, we love having Tonka and Bisbee with us. They make our house a home and, although they continue to bring us gifts of hunted birds, frogs and mice, we wouldn't change a thing about them.

When I look back at the day we went to Battersea and met these two, I wish I hadn't worried so much about taking in two cats instead of one. I am so grateful Battersea were so thorough with their vetting service. They knew before I did that Tonka and Bisbee would be perfect for Josh and me. The support and time everyone gave us, from the receptionist to the vet, were invaluable, as was being able to think overnight about taking them both. We made our decision in our own time, and in our own way. It was the best decision we ever made.

5. Molly the Sweetie

After a gruelling twelve-hour day at work, I returned to the hotel room I'd been calling home for the past three weeks and flopped on to the bed. I was a costume supervisor and my current on-location contract for a TV series was short but intense, with early starts and late finishes. I could be away for weeks at a time and it was physically and emotionally draining. Right now, there was nothing I wanted to do more than succumb to sleep, fully dressed. Even kicking off my shoes was too energy-zapping.

This trip had been even more of a rollercoaster for me because, days before, I'd lost my longest-serving companion – my beloved Whippet cross, Beni. I'd taken him in when he had been abandoned by his owners as a tiny six-week-old puppy seventeen years earlier.

While I'd been away on location, my partner Steve had moved into my home, with his two cats, to look after Beni. When my dog had suddenly become unwell, Steve had taken him to the vet and the inevitable conclusion had been reached. There was no option but to put Beni peacefully to sleep. Of course I'd known the day would come, and Beni was no spring chicken, but he'd been a scruffy, gorgeous boy with so much character and loyalty. He had lived a wonderful life, but nothing could have prepared me for the moment Steve confirmed the news to me on the phone.

I'd shaken from head to toe and my chest had felt heavy in a way I'd not experienced before. My Beni, the little scamp who would bolt away in the park and run all the way home while I searched for him frantically, my Beni, who would sit outside the house looking chuffed as anything when I returned to find him there, was gone for good.

As well as news of Beni, I had just discovered I was pregnant. It was bittersweet, knowing Beni wouldn't be there when we brought the baby home because I'd always pictured having a dog when I started a family. Now things were looking quite different. It was going to take some time to get my head around everything.

A week later, I returned home and, instead of the click-click of Beni's paws on the floor, there was nothing but silence. Then Steve appeared in the hallway and I rushed into his arms. I cried for Beni until there were no more tears to shed. I felt guilty that I hadn't been there for him at the end so had had no chance to say goodbye. But as the days turned into weeks, I realized it had been for the best that I hadn't been there when Steve had taken Beni to the vet. The thought of saying goodbye to his little face was unbearable. I doubted I'd have found the strength to do it.

Beni had been there for me through thick and thin; he'd been my constant companion through lonely times in a shared house in college while I had studied, and then been my housemate when I'd moved to London to start my career. Beni had come everywhere with me and travelled with me to wherever I'd worked. I knew for certain it would have broken me to take him to the vet myself and leave without him.

One wonderfully long chapter had ended with Beni's death but, soon, a new, thrilling chapter was about to start for Steve and me. As the tiny life inside me started to make its presence felt, I got to thinking about how my life with Steve would soon be changing. Our home would need a crib, nappies, bottles and a high chair. We'd need a pram, blankets and romper suits. We'd be up all hours taking care of the amazing new life that would soon be turning things upside down.

It was a very exciting thing to look forward to. But it would be many months before that happened and, for now, there was a certain void in our home. Even though Steve and his two cats had moved in, and my parrot, Pookha, brought colour and life to our home, without Beni, the house seemed unfamiliar.

Things simply didn't feel right without a dog.

At the weekends, I asked Steve: 'What do people do on a Sunday without a dog?'

Steve joked: 'Play with their cats?'

For seventeen years, Sunday had been the day I'd take Beni for a lovely long walk near our home in Tooting, south London, without worrying about getting to work or beating the dark hours of a winter night. On a Sunday, Beni and I had been in the park for hours without a care in the world. Now, my Sundays didn't have

Mischievous Tonka and Bisbee came as an inseparable duo from Battersea. Cheeky Tonka is seen here, eyeing up the Christmas turkey before perching halfway up the tree for a nap!

Shadow the Pug cross, who was such a comfort to his owner, Mildred, through difficult times.

Scrappie the mongrel puppy, who earned his name after he was abandoned in a park bin.

Cupid, later named Sam, became a much needed friend for lonely Lucky the Collie.

Above: Faith the Great Dane was lying emaciated and close to death in a ditch on a bitterly cold winter's day when Battersea came to her rescue.

Above: Ted finds room in his bed for Scrappie.

Right: Bailey and his new pal, Paddy, learn to play nice and share, despite their size difference.

Above: Jake the Jack Russell, who helped his owner, Mark, find purpose – and became a lifelong friend.

Below: Mark's cheeky Battersea puppy, Milo, who loves sunbathing and causing mayhem.

Above: Poppy puts an arm around loving family dog Molly.

Above and right: Molly proved to be extremely tolerant of Ruby [right] and Poppy's attempts to dress her up as Santa, or in pearls and a feather boa!

It was a dream come true for Northamptonshire police officer Emma when she was offered a job with the dog handling unit.

Herbie during specialist service dog training.

Above: Herbie's searching abilities are put to the test. *Below:* German Shepherds Prince and Tyson make the perfect candidates for prison work. They're the best of friends too.

After losing their beloved dog, Johnny Reggae (above and left), Nick and Stephanie took in another Battersea dog, Tiffin (below right). With Battersea's support, the couple helped Tiffin overcome his traumatic past.

meaning. I missed Beni terribly and I knew with certainty that I wanted another dog but, out of respect for Beni, I held on for as long as I could. Maybe it was out of a sense of loyalty. Just thinking about getting another dog made me feel I was dishonouring Beni.

Then one Sunday afternoon, I blurted out: 'Let's go to Battersea Dogs & Cats Home.'

Steve missed Beni, too, and a smile swept across his face. 'I'm ready when you are, darling,' he said.

We went to Battersea after lunch, and the Home was packed. There was a hustle and bustle of excitement, and a very tangible sense of new beginnings. I watched as couples, families and singletons came in empty-handed and emerged, some time later, with a cat-carrier or a fabulously excited dog on one of the famous blue Battersea leads. Suddenly I had a sense of urgency. I wanted to be starting a new journey.

Steve and I waited for a while and then it was our turn. We got chatting to a rehomer and I told her about Beni and how I'd had dogs all my life, from when I was a little girl, through my teenage years and now into adulthood. I told her how, in my mind's eye, I'd envisaged a shaggy dog with a friendly face and a loving personality. A dog that would slot into our little family.

After completing our interview and filling in our details, Steve and I were invited to look around the kennels but, sadly, we didn't find what we were looking for. The next weekend, we returned and were strolling around when it happened. I didn't find a dog – the dog found me.

Molly was a black mongrel, and when she spotted me, her tail began to wag. Something about her enthusiasm put a smile on my face and Steve's. Molly was six months old and as friendly as they come. I knew instantly she was going to be our new dog.

Steve and I were shown to a meeting room and had a chance to play with Molly. The rehomer also brought a friendly cat into the room so that we would get an idea of how Molly would behave with one – we had to be sure she would be good with Steve's cats. Molly glanced at the cat, which was kept safely inside a cat-carrier, then settled next to me, ignoring it entirely. She couldn't have been any less fussed by the feline intruder in our midst – the ideal reaction. After a while, the carrier was opened and, again, Molly wasn't interested. We arranged for a home visit from one of Battersea's team, and a few days later he came to see us.

As he looked around, he explained that Battersea treats every customer and the animal they would like to rehome on a case-by-case basis. 'The animal's welfare is our priority,' he said. I could see that from the meticulous assessment he carried out. He checked our garden was secure, our home had more than enough room, and asked more about my background. I told him I was an experienced dog owner, having had dogs all my life. I patted my tiny bump, and he congratulated me with a smile. 'We wouldn't necessarily recommend that parents-to-be take on a new dog,' he said, but I explained it would be several months before our baby arrived. He agreed that would be plenty of time for Molly to settle in.

'Molly had a tough time before she arrived at Battersea,' he began, 'and she has a tendency to attention-seek so be firm with her. But, despite everything she has been through, she is a remarkably content and happy dog.'

Molly had been given to Battersea because her owner's other dog didn't get along with her, but she had adapted easily to life in the kennels and was expected to settle comfortably into her new home environment. We were a perfect match for each other.

'I can see that Molly is coming to a lovely home,' the rehomer concluded. 'I don't have any concerns.'

A week later, Steve went to Battersea to pick Molly up. I waited excitedly at home and paced around the house, unable to sit down or keep still. I'd already bought her a cosy bed so I tried it in the living room by the sofa, then in the kitchen by the door and was moving it around the hallway when I heard the key in the lock. Steve appeared with a beaming smile. At his feet, a black dog was wagging her tail furiously. Steve unclipped Molly's blue Battersea lead. She bounded over to me and licked my hand. 'Hello, Molly,' I said. 'Welcome to your new home.'

Molly took stock of her surroundings and trotted to the kitchen to have a sniff around. Before I could follow her, she was back. She climbed into her bed, flopped down and snuggled in. 'Well, I guess that's her settled, then!' I said.

Steve laughed. 'Quite. At least we won't have to worry about her hiding behind the curtain or cowering away from us.'

Molly made herself at home and, very quickly, we felt as if she had been with us for ever. Next morning, we took her for a walk around Tooting Common. After a while, observing her behaviour, I said: 'Why does she keep doing that?'

'Doing what, Caroline?'

'Duck,' I said. 'She keeps ducking!'

Steve and I paid close attention and realized that whenever Molly spotted things in the sky, like a pigeon flying overhead or a frisbee whizzing by, she ducked. 'It's like she's never been outside,' I said.

We wondered if that really might have been the case. She didn't seem to have any understanding of being outside and was shocked by people, cars and noise. We guessed she had spent a lot of time indoors and hadn't really been walked or taken to a busy park. Even though she was a bit nervous on the first few walks, she soon got into the swing of them. When she began chasing pigeons, I told her: 'That's it, girl.' She'd return to me out of breath, pink tongue lolling out, and look at me as if to say: *This is quite fun, actually, Mum, isn't it?*

We noticed other things that left us scratching our heads about Molly's life before she'd come to us. Whenever Molly saw anyone in light clothing she'd rush over excitedly and try to climb up them, pawing at the person and whining softly. It made me wonder if her previous owner or perhaps someone she'd loved had often worn light colours.

We expected that our dry-cleaning bill would spike for a few weeks as we apologized to other dazed passers-by who had unexpectedly been snuffled, pawed and now had dirty marks on their jacket or jeans. 'I'm so sorry about Molly,' I'd say. 'She's just come to us from Battersea and sometimes she gets a bit overexcited. Please allow me to get that dry-cleaned that for you.' Every time, the person would graciously accept the explanation and, with a wave of their hand, dismiss the offer.

Molly hated men in helmets just as much as she liked people in light colours. With Steve working as a motor-bike courier, we learnt quickly that he should remove the helmet long before he reached our front door or Molly would go mad, barking at him.

At home, she had an altogether different quirk. She didn't know how to play.

She had no interest in toys or the games you'd expect a dog to like, such as tug of war, or a bit of rough and tumble. My brother Jonathan had a novel solution to this: whenever he came over to our house, or when we popped up the road to his, he got down on his hands and knees, took one of Molly's untouched toys in his mouth and rolled around in front of her. 'Grrr, grrrr,' he'd say, then drop the toy in front of her. 'Come on, Molly! Play! Go on, just grab it.'

Her tail was wagging because she knew this was fun, but she was still confused. *Mum, what on earth is Uncle Jon doing?* her eyes pleaded. Or perhaps she meant: *Is that what you want me to do?* I couldn't tell for sure but Molly was a clever girl. After a few dates with Jonathan, Molly got the hang of playing. I found myself repeating his tactics and, instead of looking at me as though I was mad, Molly joined in.

Molly and I were having so much fun getting to know each other that we grew incredibly close. I called her Molly the Mole because she was so black – her ears pricked up whenever I said it.

That Christmas, Steve and I travelled to my mum's house with the rest of my family. Mum's home was down in the Wiltshire countryside and she had a large garden. I couldn't figure out which excited Molly most – all the people giving her cuddles and love, or that lovely garden and the fields beyond it.

We had a busy Christmas, the house crammed with friends and family. It felt so good to get away and catch up with old schoolmates. Early every morning, I took Molly for a long walk around the fields. Now instead of ducking when something flew past her head, she chased after it. She was really coming into her own. Back at Mum's, Molly stuck to my side like my shadow but clearly enjoyed all the attention she got from everyone else.

She was so patient with my niece too. No matter how much she bumped into Molly or screamed excitedly around her, Molly didn't bat an eyelid. She was calm and moved slowly around the younger children present in a way that showed us she understood a sudden movement might frighten them. Even when they stroked Molly's fur the wrong way, she would simply shake it off and wait for the next swipe of a tiny hand. It was heart-warming to see.

Afterwards, we returned home to London and, as my bump grew and the due date loomed closer, I went through a phase of nesting. I cleaned the house from top to bottom on most days and purchased a new rug with which I felt exceptionally chuffed.

One morning I went upstairs to fetch the laundry, and when I returned to the living room, I gasped. The corner of my brand new rug had been chewed clean off! 'Molly!' I said, taking the remnants from her mouth. Firmly, I said: 'No.' Not that it dissuaded her. Molly continued chewing through the furniture, our telephone and even a remote control, but I knew from experience that a lot of young dogs were prone to it.

Sure enough, she grew out of it quickly.

In June, a rippling pain shot across my belly and snaked around my lower back. As my contractions became stronger, we dropped Molly at Jonathan's house and headed to the hospital. After hours in labour, I was taken to theatre for an emergency Caesarean section and, eventually, our beautiful little girl, Ruby, was placed in my arms. I felt an overwhelming rush of love and wanted nothing more than to take our little girl home.

After a few days on the postnatal ward, I was able to do just that. Molly was excited to see me and, after a curious sniff of Ruby, resumed normal duties, which included snoozing in bed or following me around.

Steve didn't have any paternity leave so within days I was on my own with Ruby. It wasn't easy, having just had a C-section and without my mum nearby, but I managed.

I felt a little isolated and lonely at times, as I'm sure many new mums inevitably do in the rare moments when the baby is asleep and you sit down in pure quiet. That's when a pang of loneliness hits you. It was always in those minutes that Molly would come to find me and keep me company. She was a real comfort.

There was one other problem, too. I couldn't leave the house without Steve because I couldn't get the buggy up and down the three steps to our front door because of my stitches. So I had to wait till Steve came home to take Molly for a walk with Ruby in her pram. By the time he arrived, Molly and I were equally desperate to get outside. I looked forward to those walks so much and I think Molly did too.

Steve and I strolled arm in arm with Molly on the lead trotting next to me and our darling girl asleep in her pram. I adored those summer-evening walks, and was so happy we'd made the decision to get another dog when we had. Molly was with us at the beginning of our family time together. Life simply wouldn't have been complete without her.

She got a lot out of it too. Molly learnt that the best place to sit at mealtimes was next to Ruby in her high-chair, a prime carrot-purée-catching spot. Molly got covered with whatever Ruby was eating, and it wasn't long before they both twigged that it was good fun. While they were in league together, I was left to clear up the mess the naughty twosome had made but, truthfully, I didn't mind.

When Ruby was three we had another daughter, Poppy, and as the girls grew, the games continued. I'd often be in another room in the house when I'd hear their giggles.

Then one of the girls would come to find me and, tugging impatiently on my sleeve, say: 'Come and look, Mum.'

I'd follow her into the other room where I'd find Molly sitting quietly, her glittering fairy wings only outdone by the string of sparkling beads and feather boa around her neck. The girls would be falling about laughing and Molly would look at me with what might have been a frown: *Please help me, Mum.*

But Molly loved the attention and she knew after the game of dress-up, something even better would follow: fetch, in the garden. By now we'd moved to a bigger house with a large garden for Molly and the girls. Ruby and Poppy took turns to throw the ball and Molly would leap to catch it, returning it to whichever sister was standing closer to her. She was instinctively gentle with them, and didn't care when either girl was only able to throw it a few feet. She just loved them playing with her.

Jonathan liked spending time at ours, and made the decision to get a dog, too. Off he went to Battersea and, soon after, brought home a Spaniel cross with white and black markings. His name was Parker, and he got on with Molly like a house on fire.

Jonathan, his wife, Margie, their son, Charlie, Steve, the girls and I often packed our bags and drove all over the country for camping holidays. The kids and the dogs loved the trips away and so did we. We were in Wales one year when I woke in the very early hours with a sense of panic. Steve was frantically searching for something and his urgency – and noisy way of moving about and jostling the camp bed – had woken me.

'What are you doing?' I said.

'We have to find Molly – she's gone.'

I jumped out of bed and pulled on my boots as Steve started calling her in that loud whispering kind of way.

Suddenly there was a burst of laughter.

I raced out to find Steve clutching his sides as Jonathan appeared, half dressed, with a sheepish Molly at his side. Across the burnt-out fire he said: 'If you're looking for your dog, she woke me up at three o'clock and has been camped in our tent all night!'

It turned out she'd found the zip keeping her inside our tent, nudged it up and sneaked out, then dashed across to Jonathan's when she'd got spooked. He'd found her cuddled up with Parker.

After we'd finished laughing, I got to thinking. I told Steve my idea and he agreed we should get Molly a playmate. She had the softest temperament and got on with every dog she met but, lately, I'd noticed something about her. I wasn't the only one to see it. Ruby said: 'Molly doesn't like to play any more.'

She was right.

Our parrot, Pookha, regularly teased Molly by sneaking up and nibbling her, but Molly had become quite lazy and wouldn't chase her off. She spent hours lying about. It felt like the right time for her and the girls to have a new friend.

Poppy was mad about dogs, and Steve and I agreed that while she was still young enough to enjoy it, we should thinking about getting a young dog. I found myself looking at the dogs that needed homes on the Battersea website. I scanned the pictures and profiles and thought: *Are you the one we're looking for?*

Deep down, I'd set my heart on a Petit Basset Griffon Vendéen, a small, shaggy dog known for its friendly demeanour and I'd met a few on our camping trips. Months passed, and none was available for rescue at Battersea or any other rescue centre. These dogs rarely came up for adoption because the families who were lucky enough to have one hardly ever gave it up. I wanted to rehome another dog, but we were not finding what we were looking for and time was getting on.

Then we had a stroke of luck. I heard that a local lady's Basset had unexpectedly had puppies, which needed rehoming. I contacted her and we got chatting. She had two puppies left. 'Why don't you come and meet them?'

'I'd love to,' I said.

When I dropped by, the lady showed me to the garden where, in a fenced-off area, two fluffy brown and white puppies were playing in the sunshine. I crouched down and they both came to say hello. Within a few seconds, one puppy had plonked itself down a few feet away and was looking around, but the other remained right next to me, nibbling my hand and waiting for more strokes. He was a lot like Molly had been at that age: friendly, curious and very loving. But I could also tell he was a bit of a scamp and very playful, like Beni had been as a puppy.

The puppy had stolen my heart, but I told his owner: 'I need to discuss this with my partner.'

On the way home, I called Steve and told him all about the meeting, and the lovely puppy. 'This is going to be a really good thing for Molly,' he said.

It seemed like Molly's destiny.

A week later, I picked up the puppy and we named him Hector. Molly, as usual, took everything in her stride. She sniffed him and he sniffed her. Hector took a couple of steps back and forward, jiggling around in front of her. Molly looked at me. *Is that all he does, Mum?* And then she went straight to her bed.

Hector, however, was more curious about Molly. He followed her into bed, climbed on her back and tumbled down the other side. Molly didn't so much as flinch and was soon fast asleep, with Hector still rolling around her. It was a relief to see how easily she'd taken to him – no fuss or bother. I knew then I'd made the right choice.

Hours later, Ruby arrived home from school. I had wanted Hector to be a surprise so I held back a grin as I waited for her to notice him. She was telling me about her day when she clocked Hector in Molly's bed. Her eyes snapped back to me. 'Oh!' she said. 'What's that puppy doing here?'

'He's ours,' I told her. 'Do you like him?'

Ruby nodded furiously, then ran across the room to have a closer look.

Moments later, Poppy came in and when she spotted what her sister was looking at, she gasped. 'Are we looking after him?'

I nodded.

'Do we have to take him back?'

This time I shook my head. 'Hector is here to stay.'

The girls were so excited that it took a while for the news to sink in. None of us could stop smiling.

For the next few weeks, Hector was too little to run around with Molly but as he grew, she chased him around the garden. Hector teased her by nabbing her favourite ball and running away with it. For years, Molly had been quiet and not much of a barker. Now she was barking with excitement in the garden on most days, and there were times when I wanted to stop her running around. 'She'll have a heart attack at this rate!' I told Steve.

The truth was that Hector had given Molly a new lease of life, just as we'd hoped would be the case.

As a child, I had always had a dog and I'm so glad Steve and I have been able to provide the same fun and joy for our children. My mum used to say: 'A child must have a dog to play with.'

I couldn't agree more. It teaches them about life and

death, caring and loss. It brings life lessons big and small and, for me, part of having a home is having a dog. I'd like to think the girls feel the same way.

Molly and Hector have enriched our lives and our family doesn't feel complete unless we're all together.

Poppy wants to be a vet when she grows up and I'm happy that her upbringing may shape her future in such a tangible, positive way.

6. New Beginnings

The Life of a Service Dog

As the sunlight bathed my skin, I took a step back and looked at the field before me. I was a police officer and, having spent years on the front line, at that moment I was one step closer to my dream.

My mentor handed me a lead. 'This time, you track the field, Emma.'

Before I had a chance to react, the lead in my hand became taut and the German Shepherd at the end charged forward. Malley, a general-purpose police dog and one of the best with Northamptonshire Police, expertly manoeuvred around the training field, tracking footprints and items of clothing that had been planted hours earlier by my mentor Pete to replicate the work required on a crime scene.

Pete was a legend in the field of training special dogs like Malley, and had taken me under his wing in the hope that one day I would become a dog handler too. I felt privileged indeed. We moved quickly around the field, Malley pulling me forward, picking up clothes and other clues along the way.

'So that's what it feels like to be one of a team,' I said to Pete, when we'd completed the course.

He laughed. 'Yes, something like that.'

In that moment, I wanted the job more than anything in the world.

I continued training with Pete in my spare time, using my leave days to build my knowledge and learn key skills in preparation for when a vacancy might come up on the dog-handling unit. I watched Pete train his dog and he showed me what it meant to take on this lifestyle. Because that was what it was – a lifestyle, as much as a job. Malley was Pete's dog for work and at the end of each shift he took her home with him. That special relationship between a handler and their dog was one of the many reasons officers lucky enough to join the team rarely left.

After five years, I had my chance. When the vacancy bulletin went out for a new member of the dog unit in our force, I was one of fifty officers to apply. There was a written application, fitness tests and exams, then an interview. In my time with the force, I'd worked on everything from the Criminal Investigation Department, automobile crimes, the ANPR (Automatic Number Plate Reader) team, drug crimes and as acting sergeant, and hoped my experience would give me an edge over the others, who were just as eager to get the job. I went into that interview armed with knowledge and experience but with a bellyful of butterflies.

I was the lucky one.

I soon met the dog who would be my full-time partner, a German Shepherd called Willis. We trained together for twelve weeks, learning all the skills we needed before we were operational and ready to go out on calls, although Willis would receive continual training throughout his career.

The work was everything I had dreamt it would be. Willis and I went to all sorts of jobs, from burglaries to crime scenes to searching for a missing person. It was exciting and exhilarating.

Eighteen months passed and my line manager told me I would be taking on a second dog, this time a specialist dog that sniffed out drugs, arms or large quantities of money. It was likely to be a Springer Spaniel because the breed is especially well suited to the work. A Springer's obedient temperament and their hard-working nature make them perfect for what we had in mind. This time I would help to search for the right dog.

I sat down with my iPad, pulled up a new search on Google and typed in 'rescue dogs'. Then I read about the centres near Northamptonshire Police HQ. When my search yielded no results, I began to look at breeders. I made dozens of calls and told everyone I came into contact with that we were on the lookout for our newest recruit.

Two weeks later, no closer to finding my new partner, something occurred to me.

I returned to Google and typed in 'Battersea Dogs & Cats Home'. As I clicked through the various pages of the website, I came across Keith Payne, the service dog manager for the Home.

I rang Keith to hear a bit more about Battersea's service dog programme. I learnt that, from the thousands of dogs that come to the Home's three sites each year, the team at Battersea keep an eye out for particularly smart dogs who love to play ball or tug games, and are between six months and four years old.

Some breeds have inherent traits that make them excel in certain fields – for instance, the Rottweiler's strength, guarding instinct and confidence make them excellent security dogs. Keith told me Border Collies, Springer and Cocker Spaniels and Labradors were often at the top of his list, too, and he looked for confident, outgoing and physically fit dogs. Some were scouted for farm or security work but many breeds have the potential to become part of the service dog programme.

Keith explained that Battersea recognizes that many of the dogs that eventually go to 'service homes' display behaviour that makes them unsuitable for a traditionally domestic home, and they need the stimulus of a happy working life. The benefits and rewards, for dogs and owners, are immeasurable so Battersea pick their service dogs as though they are choosing a candidate for a top job.

I told Keith my requirements, and he said: 'We've actually just taken in a Springer Spaniel.' Though the dog was only six months old, too young for our type of specialist training, I reckoned he was worth a look after Keith had explained he'd been through the normal ten or more sessions to assess his potential and been identified as a good candidate for service work.

'When can we see him?' I asked.

The next day, my colleague Greg and I climbed into a

police van and drove along the motorway to Battersea Old Windsor. We got stuck in traffic, and a journey that should have taken just over an hour took three. When we arrived, Keith gave us a tour of the site and took us to the kennels. We passed a dozen dogs and arrived at the kennel with our candidate inside.

Herbie was bouncing up and down, itching to get out. Keith clipped on a lead and brought him over, then handed him to me. We went outside and headed to the training area in a large enclosed garden. By now, Herbie had stopped bouncing and was almost shy. He waited by my side and I could sense he felt a bit overwhelmed by all the sights and sounds. I wondered if he was too young for what we had in mind. The dogs needed a level of maturity and discipline to become the best possible police dog. Was Herbie cut out for the job?

Keith set up a search in an upstairs room by hiding a tennis ball while we waited in the garden. He called us up, then turned to Herbie. 'Search.'

With that, Herbie was off, searching the boxes and cupboards at such speed, I wondered if he could possibly be doing a thorough job. He raced through the room like a whirlwind! But, sure enough, within a few minutes, he returned with a yellow tennis ball.

Greg's and my eyebrows shot up. Herbie was clearly a star.

'I think Herbie has great potential,' I told Greg.

He nodded in agreement and we took a walk and chatted about the dog. We discussed his age and decided that, although it might go against him in training, he was still worth taking on, even if we ended up keeping him back until he was a year old and ready to train. I told Keith: 'We'll take him.'

A month later, in July 2013, I went to pick Herbie up. I drove to Old Windsor in my police-dog van and took Willis with me in one of the two cages in the back. When I arrived, whether or not he remembered me, Herbie seemed happy to see me. His eyes were bright and his tail was wagging at full speed. I loaded him into the cage next to Willis's and the two were able to have a whiff of one another. I wouldn't introduce them properly for a few weeks, instead letting them slowly familiarize themselves with each other. In that way, they could get used to their new dynamic before Herbie started his full training course. We wanted him to settle in a bit.

The first week was tough. Herbie was anxious and didn't settle well at night: he howled and cried through the early hours. His kennel and Willis's were in the garden: they were working dogs, and had to understand that when they entered a building they would do so to work and search. Also, they would be safe outside in their kennel from anyone who happened across them by accident, and, of course, they needed somewhere of their own to relax and unwind.

Night after night, I ended up out there keeping Herbie company. I knew he was adapting to a new environment for the third time in his short life and it was a lot to get used to for such a young puppy. He began biting and chewing the bars on his kennel so I

'Herbified' everything with metal panels. I worried we'd made a mistake in picking him but hoped that, in time, he'd settle in. Willis didn't seem to mind all the noise – he slept right through it.

During the day, I made friends with Herbie and tried extra hard to bond with him. We played games and I spent a lot of time with him, just the two of us. I desperately wanted Herbie to trust me and form with me the same special bond I had with Willis, and I knew from experience that the best way to achieve that was to play with him. I also knew that, ultimately, Herbie and any other specially trained dog wouldn't work for me if they didn't have that bond. It's the bond that fuels the working world we're in and dogs like Herbie want to please their mum or dad, get rewarded and be in that constant cycle of positivity.

So, I spent time with Herbie at home, playing with him, taking him out and giving him constant love and reassurance. When he messed on the floor I trained him to stop by rewarding his good behaviour, rather than telling him off.

After a month, Herbie had settled down, becoming less nervy, and we grew much closer. Pete came over and, together, we took Willis and Herbie to neutral ground – a cricket pitch nearby. We planned to do a controlled meeting and would break things up if they got out of hand. I had been a little apprehensive but Willis was brilliant. Pete and I sat down and started throwing balls to the dogs. While Pete focused on Willis, I took care of Herbie. Before long, the two dogs had forgotten about Pete and me and were chasing each other on the field. They got on brilliantly.

While they played, Pete and I chatted. I learnt that, in the past, our dog unit had taken on puppies but usually we placed them in training at twelve or fourteen months old. Herbie was seven months and I wondered when I should start training him. Given that he had settled in at home, we decided to get him started on the Specialist Search Dog Training Course, which allowed him to train with several things, including drugs.

Our initial sessions only reinforced the good signs we'd picked up weeks earlier at Battersea. Herbie had a strong drive to search which we tested by hiding his tennis ball in a room. He quickly figured out there was a game to be had, and that is essential for dogs in the police force. It's the best way to train them.

Luckily for us, Herbie was very ball driven and flew through the course. As the training progressed, we tested his skill in identifying odours and trained him to sniff out drugs.

We started off on the one with the most potent smell – amphetamine.

Herbie was trained as a passive indicating dog: he would freeze and stare at the place where he detected the scent of the drugs, cash or firearms. This was so that he would not interfere with the substances when he found them, while also significantly reducing any risks to himself.

Herbie took to the process like a duck to water. Whenever he smelt the drug he was looking for, his eyebrows shot up, his tail began to wag and he'd let out a bark. If there had been a thought bubble above his head it would have read: *Ooh! There's that smell – and, ooh! Here's my ball!*

After that, we were able to drag the process out a bit so that Herbie learnt to sit and wait when he found something. He soon caught on. In a remarkably short time, he was able to identify heroin, ecstasy, cocaine and crack, as well as the original amphetamine, and was ready for his Home Office Assessment.

He passed with flying colours, which meant he was ready to be out on the streets getting his paws dirty.

Herbie was the youngest dog we'd ever brought on to Northamptonshire Police's dog section, which had a sergeant, an inspector, two trainers and ten handlers like me. Time would tell how successful he would be.

On our first shift, as I stood ready in the police courtyard with Herbie, who was wearing a special harness to go out on a search, I had to pinch myself to believe I was really doing this for a living. Even after three years, it was still such a thrill.

As our van set off, Herbie was comfortably snoozing in the back, as was Willis. Both dogs came with me wherever I went when I was working, and while I was out with one dog, the other waited for his turn.

Herbie was a bit nervous when I put the siren on but he recognized quickly that the noisy thing on the roof meant he was going to do exciting things outside the van and he soon got used it.

He got into the swing of our shift patterns, and

when I worked overtime, so did he. As long as that harness was on, Herbie was in work mode – professional, thorough and always paying full attention. He was the model employee.

Soon after, we were sent to search for drugs in a house linked with criminal activity.

Every inch of the place was crammed with rubbish and mess. I looked at it and thought: *Where do I start looking?* Using our training, we searched each room methodically. I knew if anything was there, Herbie would find it.

Every twenty minutes, we stopped for Herbie to take a break because that's the amount of time it took for him to get nasal fatigue, which meant his breathing pattern changed, causing him to pant. This would make him less efficient and more likely to miss a substance he was searching for. After a walk round outside and a bit of time relaxing, Herbie was ready again.

He got stuck in and, later, indicated there was something by the fireplace, which was filled with ash. On top of the ash was a burnt purse: Herbie flicked it on to the floor and indicated again.

I rewarded him with his ball but wondered if he was just playing with me. When I began looking through the purse, I gasped. Hidden inside, I found six wraps of heroin.

Next, Herbie indicated on the grate, sending a cloud of ash into the air with his snout. I rewarded him again, and began sifting through the ash while on my hands and knees.

Herbie had this look on his face that said: *Keep digging, go on, it's in there!*

Sure enough, I found more heroin wraps. I pulled out so many that it was like panning for gold! In the end I counted fifty. It was a phenomenal find for Herbie over four hours. I knew I was biased about what a wonderful dog he was but I was bursting with pride. Herbie was turning out to be an excellent police dog.

That wasn't his only successful search. We trained him up to find firearms and cash, and this year alone, he has been part of some of the biggest cash seizures our dog section has ever seen. So far, Herbie's biggest finds have included £50,000, £100,000 and £33,000 cash, along with 2.5 kilos of Class A drugs, all linked to an organized-crime group. There were times when he would even sniff out a single ten-pound note. I was amazed at how accurate his skills were. Training him so young was not an issue.

As soon as we returned home and Herbie's harness came off, he was just like any other dog. He and Willis chased each other around the garden, dug up all my plants and made a complete mess. Despite our close working relationship, Herbie had some trouble learning to trust me. He was hand-shy: if I went to stroke him and caught him off guard, he'd cower away from me or pee. I could see that, deep down, he was a delicate, sensitive soul, and whatever had happened to him before he'd gone to Battersea had left an emotional mark on him.

His previous owners had documented behaviour

problems, and at Battersea, Herbie had initially been a little submissive, which isn't unusual for a dog in a new environment with unfamiliar noise, people and loads of other dogs. That was why I made sure that all the training for work was done away from home. I wanted Herbie to understand that when he came home it was time for love, play and cuddles.

I was gentle with him when I needed to be and spent time getting to know him and helping him forge a friendship with Willis. At the weekends, I took them both down to the river for a walk near our home in Northamptonshire and they'd dive in and have a swim before finding and soaking me. Then they'd charge off together round the countryside.

Being around Willis, who loved and trusted me unconditionally, definitely helped Herbie: he became more confident around me. He no longer jumped when I went to stroke him or moved suddenly. That wasn't the only change I saw in our little family: Willis became more playful and seemed to have taken on a new lease of life with his friend around.

I don't think Herbie will ever be a bold dog but he was born to work. I can work with him all day long, like a Duracell bunny, and he loves the job. Yet he comes home, stands in my flowerbeds, barks at cats and, despite failing miserably, still believes he will one day catch a squirrel.

Herbie and Willis are happy, silly souls at home, and Herbie has come out of his shell. Like many Springers, he's a real live wire. He has boundless energy, and I've nicknamed him Herbie the Hooligan. He's always digging things up, generally doing naughty things and egging Willis on. They're crackers sometimes. I watch them wrestling over a toy and think, *Are they really police dogs?*

Hours later, they're out doing serious police work to the highest standard.

But their world is simple. Love, work, play.

Herbie's life is a bit of a modern day fairy tale. He ended up at Battersea when he was just a few months old and he needed a home. His knight in shining armour – Keith – tapped into his skills, and now Herbie is a successful operational police dog, with a loving home, a mum and a brother.

For Herbie, this is his happily ever after.

Recruiting

I sat at my desk at work and sighed with frustration. It was my job as custodial manager for the dog section to supervise the handlers, control the budget and find new dogs to join our team – but it wasn't always easy recruiting them.

I was on the lookout for dogs that wanted to be doing something all the time. They were the ones that did not make ideal pets and often misbehaved. I'd learnt over the years to look for the hooligans that nobody else wanted – the Springer Spaniel that had destroyed a three-seater sofa in a matter of hours, the German

Shepherd that had ripped up thirty square metres of carpet in a day. Those were the dogs I looked for because, often, they were perfect for service dog roles.

Eleven years ago, when I began working for the prison service, it had been much easier to find those dogs because only the police, the prison service and the army were looking for them. Now, as I trawled through the websites of animal-rescue centres and made dozens of calls, I realized that there weren't enough dogs out there with potential to be trained up to cater for all the services that wanted them.

At our prison alone, we had a minimum of three dogs patrolling the perimeter twenty-four hours a day, seven days a week, 365 days a year, with a fourth dog resting and ready to take over so the others could have a break. With private security firms willing to pay massive amounts of money for the right dogs, the pool available to us was getting smaller and smaller.

We'd also learnt the hard way that our dogs needed social skills: they were often working side by side and needed to get on with other dogs in the unit. It was quite a wish list but one day I had an idea.

One of my team typed a letter and when it was done he posted a copy to every rescue organization nearby to remind them of what we were always looking out for. We repeated this every other month to keep the dialogue going. One day I received a call from Keith Payne, the service dog manager at Battersea Dogs & Cats Home. 'We have a young German Shepherd here. He's two years old and he might be what you're looking for.'

'What makes you think he's right for us?'

Keith explained: 'Tyson is a very ball-driven dog and he's happy to search for it on command.'

My ears pricked up: rewarding our dogs with a ball was the basis of all our training.

Keith added: 'He also has a reasonable amount of defence drive in him.'

That was music to my ears. 'We can come and see him in two days' time. Is that OK with you?'

Our meeting was set. That Friday, my lead trainer, Del, and I made the short drive from Thamesmead, south-east London, to Battersea Old Windsor to meet Tyson. Keith introduced us and we took Tyson for a walk around the grounds. We'd gone wearing our full uniform, which was all black, on purpose because sometimes dogs didn't like men dressed in black. The reason for this is unknown but it can cause fearful and adverse reactions in them.

We were pleased that Tyson didn't show any reaction to it. He was happy to let us walk him and had no qualms about meeting new people – another good sign.

Keith took him from us and slipped off his lead in a field on site that was dedicated to training dogs. 'Let me show you what he can do.'

We hid the ball and Tyson knew to look for it when we asked him to. Then we gave Keith a padded sleeve and encouraged Tyson to grab it, which he did. The bite training was essential for any dog we recruited. In time we'd encourage the dog to grab the pad and have a game of tug of war. We'd build on it until he was desperate to have a go.

Keith had already done the pad work with Tyson, a real bonus for us. Next, we watched Tyson have a run around to check that his gait was right and that he was a fit and healthy dog. German Shepherds are sometimes prone to hip problems and can be hip scored – a visual check of their gait as they walk and run in puppyhood to see if they are likely to develop problems in that area later.

Next we watched Keith put Tyson through his paces with agility tests, such as jumping a three-foot hurdle. Though Tyson hadn't done that before, he leapt over the equipment Keith had to hand with no problem.

'This one is a natural,' I told Del.

We were seriously impressed, so we took Tyson with us that day to meet his new handler.

Our unit had thirty patrol dogs and eight search dogs, each with their own handler. There was one person I thought would be perfect for Tyson. Ian was one of my most experienced handlers and his patrol dog, Prince, was eight years old and ready for early retirement as he'd developed a limp. It was standard practice for us to retire the dogs early for health reasons so they'd enjoy a good quality of life. More than that, Ian was a full service patrol-dog handler, living on his own with Prince in the countryside. He was the perfect candidate to take on a second dog.

But there was a bit of a problem because it was late December and therefore it would be difficult to arrange the standard eight-week training course straight away for Tyson and Ian to complete together, with so many people off work for the Christmas holidays. I handed Tyson over to Ian anyway so that the two could get to know each other. As Christmas set in, Tyson's journey began . . .

The Unshakeables

It was a busy Monday afternoon and as the rush-hour commuters piled on to the bus I was driving, it dawned on me that I hated my job. The writing had been on the wall for a while and it was time for a change.

I picked up a newspaper on my way home and it was then that an advert caught my eye. I applied for a job in the prison service and I was hired. I started working on discipline duties with the inmates and, after a while, I had my eye on another job, within the prison this time: a dog handler working patrols.

The job would be perfect for me. My family had always kept dogs, and I'd wanted one of my own for a long time, but because I was single and worked full time, I couldn't have one. The only way I could have a dog of my own was to join the dog unit where the dog would come home with me when my shift ended.

I began visiting the training grounds on my lunch breaks and got to know the team, always hoping a vacancy would pop up. Two years later, in 1995, an internal memo circulated, advertising a dog-handler job. I went for it and got it.

The two years I'd spent being a thorn in the unit's side – always asking them questions, tagging along to training sessions, visiting for updates on job vacancies – had finally paid off.

My life changed and I couldn't have been happier.

A few years after I'd started at HMP Pentonville, rumours surfaced that the dog section was going to close. In time, the rumour proved true, and I was transferred to HMP Belmarsh's dog section, working a shift pattern for thirty-nine hours a week. The dog assigned to me was two-and-a-half-year-old Prince, a steely German Shepherd: he had been found in Ireland, running around and worrying sheep, then brought to England where we'd taken him on. As we got to know him, we reckoned Prince had escaped from the army because if you put an angry man in front of him he knew to go and bite him. He knew how to leave – stop – when told to, and walked to heel. He was 80 per cent trained already, but without a microchip or a tattoo in his ear identifying him, we couldn't find out any more about him.

He trained up very quickly and was a great dog to have on patrol. He was always calm, alert and did as he was told. At home, he was like any other dog, partial to treats and barking at dogs on the TV. Every Sunday I treated him to a full roast dinner. Whatever I cooked for myself that day, Prince would have a bowl too. I reasoned that if I had to live on dry food and biscuits all my life, I wouldn't be very happy. Anyway, I liked to treat him.

After years of pining for a dog of my own, I had one to spoil. Prince was great company and very loyal. He loved to run and play, and kept me fit, walking the fields near our home and spending long afternoons by the river. It was nice to have company and Prince and I my formed a very special bond. I was never without him in waking hours and he became an extension of me.

At night, like all other dogs on the unit, he slept in his kennel in the garden. During work hours, he was an excellent prison-patrol dog and wasn't fazed by anything. He was extremely intuitive, and if I felt him tense up while we were patrolling through the courtyard where the prisoners exercised, I knew an altercation between inmates was about to occur. He was the perfect early-warning system.

When Prince was eight years old, I noticed he was limping. I took him to the vet and found he had developed arthritis in his hips. With us walking miles every day on the job, there was only one option. We set a plan to let Prince retire, and it was then that my line manager, Stuart, told me about a rescue dog called Tyson. He thought Tyson would be a perfect replacement for Prince on the job. Of course, Prince would remain with me at home after his retirement, but while he was still working, I took Tyson to the prison every day to begin an orientation process. At first, I kept the dogs apart, walking them separately before and after work. It was tiring but it had to be done that way. It can be difficult integrating a new German Shepherd into a home where one already lives and I was worried about how Tyson and Prince would get on when they finally met. It wouldn't have been a surprise if they had hated each other for a while or if one had tried to lead the other.

To give them time to get used to the idea of each other, I took them both to work every day in the back of my dog van. They were able to get used to the other's smell and saw each other briefly when I took one of them out.

During shifts, when Prince was having a half-hour rest, I took Tyson around the grounds, getting him familiar with things. Our formal training was yet to begin but this was a good test. A month passed, and the dogs showed no signs of hostility towards each other, only curiosity. One morning at four a.m., as I waited for our shift to begin, we were on neutral ground outside the prison: I let them both out of the van to meet. They said hello and, after a whiff of each other, sat down by my feet with their tails and tongues wagging. Their expressions said the same thing: *Father, look at him!*

Luckily, Tyson and Prince got on with each other from day one. There wasn't a cross word between them, and that was a relief. Now, instead of walking each dog separately, I was able to take them for walks together and the two got on like a house on fire. They ran around, played and chased each other. In the garden, they curled up for a sleep together and it was rather endearing to see those big prison dogs turn into such soppy souls.

Meanwhile, as Tyson became accustomed to his new surroundings at work, he was quick to learn that as soon as we arrived for our shift outside the prison walls it was game on. He was instantly alert, ready to work and excited to get in there. I tried him on the slippery floors, working at height, solid and metal stairs, and he ran around like he owned the place. Tyson wasn't fazed by anything. There wasn't a single object we put in his way that made him say: *I'm not very happy about this.*

Tyson was fearless, and in the first two weeks, I was able to walk him through the jail with all the loud and buzzing security doors, metal stairs, around the big and echoing gym, in the wet showers, and I could see that he was cut out for the job. He didn't flinch at anything. Tyson dragged me up and down narrow stairs without an ounce of hesitation, and if prisoners were acting suspiciously, he wasn't scared of them. In fact, if I threw a ball into the crowd, he was happy to go after it.

Everything was a new experience for him and he lapped it up. I was seeing in him all the same unshakeable qualities that I had seen in Prince. I knew he would make an excellent patrol dog.

Over the Christmas period, Tyson, Prince and I all worked shifts as usual. It is usually a difficult time for the prisoners, who are away from their families, and they want it to be over as quickly as possible, although they are allowed more visits than usual. Because of that, it's a busy and relentless time for staff. The risk of self-harm is increased and patrols are more important than ever.

On Christmas Day, we worked an early shift and the dogs were with me. As the official training course hadn't started yet, Tyson went out on patrol with me. It worked well to continue his orientation, especially with the added tension among the prisoners, but also because it gave Prince a chance to rest as Tyson picked up more of his patrols.

We finished in the early afternoon and returned home together, where our own Christmas Day finally began. I cooked a turkey with all the trimmings: bacon, roast potatoes, and vegetables. The boys and I had a full Christmas dinner and then the three of us settled in the lounge to open some presents.

They had giant bone-shaped chews wrapped in Christmas paper, and as they got stuck into them, I couldn't help but laugh. I was turning into a complete softie, wrapping up presents for my dogs! But Tyson and Prince seemed to be enjoying it as much as I was. I didn't have a partner to spend Christmas with or a big family, but Prince and Tyson made it as special as if I'd had a dinner table full of close friends and relatives. Prince was used to Christmases like these, but I had no idea what Tyson's background had been. I wished I could find out more. That wasn't an option so I did what I could for it to be Tyson's best Christmas yet. I spoilt them both with games and long walks over the frosty fields.

Two weeks into the New Year, Tyson and I were finally able to get started on the official training course. He did exceptionally well and mastered all the phases of training with ease. The only thing we had trouble with was getting him to bark. It was then that we were able to surmise that, at some point, Tyson had been kept as a pet because he'd obviously been taught to be quiet. It was a hard habit to break, but barking was vital in his role. Patrol dogs need to be able to bark on demand for crowd control or when they find something we need to investigate, contraband or otherwise. Once he'd understood he could make a noise, he didn't look back.

Tyson flew through the course, passed his initial licence and was soon working full shifts. Prince went into retirement and couldn't wait to see us when we got home. Whenever he had a mad moment and ran in circles around Tyson, Tyson looked to me with confusion on his face: *Are you sure about him, Father?* He loved it, really. Even after a long day's work, he was soon caught up in Prince's energy. Every day when I got home, I put the boys on their leads and headed out for a long walk.

The pair of them had a thing about cats: as soon as we were outside, they were no longer going for a walk but scanning every corner for felines. The moment either of them caught a whiff of an unsuspecting moggy, they yanked me forward – it took all my strength not to fall flat on my face as my arms were stretched out and I looked like Ben-Hur being pulled along on his chariot!

Soon, we'd be on to the fields near my home and I'd let the boys off their leads. They loved being out in the open and expended so much energy running around that, by the time we got in, they were ready for a sleep. At night, Tyson slept in his kennel in the garden, like Prince once had, but now that Prince was retired he

stayed indoors with me. If I was off work and out without the dogs, they were both kept in kennels because
of their special training. I couldn't take any risks with
them. When I was out with both of them, I realized
there was a bit of a stigma attached to the breed. People
would cross the road so they didn't have to pass me and
seemed frightened of Prince and Tyson. However, I
had only to walk 150 yards from my home before we
were in the fields, and most people in the area knew
that the dogs were under my control.

At work, Tyson excelled. One day, he and I were
watching the inmates on an exercise break in the yard
when a scuffle broke out. One inmate was attacking
another. As per our regulations, dog handlers like me
are not allowed to intervene in the initial stages. Just as
he'd been trained, Tyson went to the end of his lead
and barked continuously until the scuffle broke up.
He'd executed the textbook response and I reckoned it
was a good indication that he'd do all right in the job.
It's part of our duty to make our presence felt but we're
not allowed on to the yard. Our main role is to remind
the inmates we're there and that if they don't behave
we'll be on their heels.

The minute we were out of the prison after a shift,
Tyson's whole demeanour changed. He'd see Prince
and say: *Look, there's my friend and I'm going to run around
with him.* They would be very excited until we got out of
the door.

Now, Tyson has been doing this job for nearly a year
and has matured into it really well. Every spring, there

is a local prison-dog trial and handlers are asked to compete in it and really push the dogs. They're judged by a member of the inspectorate, then go on to the national trials. Tyson competed in May this year. He didn't win but he came very close to claiming the Criminal Work Trophy.

Just like Prince before him, Tyson makes me proud every day. Without rescue centres like Battersea, wonderfully bright and capable dogs like him would be with people who didn't understand them and, therefore, would never realize their full potential. I'm so grateful he's ended up with Prince and me.

7. Bringing our Home to Life

Any mother who has seen her children fly the nest will know the mixture of pride and pain that it causes, the sudden silence in the house. There is no laundry that must be done before the school week starts and no time by which dinner must be on the table. Life takes on an altogether different pace.

Years earlier, I might have yearned for a night off to have a long soak in the bath with a glass of wine. But now that my sons Derek and David had grown up and moved out, I longed for the chaos, noise and bustle that two young children generated. But the boys had left a piece of them with me: our Staffie cross, Venger.

He'd come into our lives unexpectedly. One day, teenage Derek came home from school and talked excitedly about a friend who had a dog that needed a new home. I was friends with the boy's mother and knew she was having a very tough time. Life had dealt her a difficult hand and, to top it off, her puppy was ripping everything to shreds, from skirting boards to clothes.

When Derek and then David pleaded with me to take the dog, I'd caved in. Venger came into our lives and carried on shredding everything in his path. He chewed the table legs and anything wooden he could get his teeth into. One night, I dabbed oil of cloves on all the wood at Venger height. The next morning, I watched as he grabbed a chair leg for a chew, winced, shook his head, then spat and spat. That was the last time he ever chewed anything but his food and toys.

The boys loved having a dog around and spent hours with him. They played fetch in the garden and down at the park, as well as tug of war if the mood took them. When they were fourteen, they had wanted to walk the dog but at sixteen they were no longer keen – they wanted to go out with their friends – so it fell to Terry and me to walk Venger.

He very much became our dog. Terry and I worked for the same employer, Terry full time as a maintenance manager and I part time on the shop floor, so we managed to establish a routine with Venger. Terry took him out in the morning and I walked him in the afternoon.

The boys had long since moved out when, one day, Venger collapsed. He was old and grey, nearing the end of his life. I knew the time to say goodbye would soon be upon us – it was just a matter of when. I took him to the vet, fearing the worst, but she prescribed some tablets for his spleen. I felt a rush of relief. We still had some time together.

As we chatted, the vet, who was lovely, an Australian called Lucia, told me about another Staffie cross. 'Buster was abandoned by his owners and we've been taking care of him. We've treated him for prostate cancer but I can't keep him with me much longer.'

I thought back to the friend who'd given Venger to us. 'What's the problem?'

'I've got a cat. Buster and she aren't getting along,' she replied. 'It's not ideal for him to stay with me any more.'

While she continued checking Venger over, I nipped outside to the car where Terry was waiting. I told him about Buster. 'What do you think?'

'I know what *you're* thinking and I don't see why not.'

I went back inside and told Lucia that I had a solution for her. 'We'll take Buster home with us.'

Lucia's face lit up and mine did the same. I'd gone in expecting to say goodbye to Venger and now I was returning not only with him but Buster too.

Now that Venger was older and didn't care too much for long walks, we took him out first for a short one and returned to take Buster for a longer one. But over the next week, something odd happened. Suddenly Venger was livelier.

'Is it just me or is Venger being a bit competitive?' I asked Terry.

'I didn't think the old boy had it in him but, yes, I think you're right, Pat,' he agreed.

It was a side to Venger we hadn't seen before.

By this time Venger didn't much like playing but he huffed and puffed when Buster bounded around him. He vied for our attention, and our home lit up with the energy Buster had brought to it.

We took the boys everywhere with us, whether it was on a walk to the bakery around the corner or to the park for a stroll in the afternoon. I realized how much I'd missed mothering someone, taking care of them and worrying about their food or clearing up after them.

Derek lived far away but David popped in when he could, and he had the energy to roll around and play with the dogs. It was then I began to see that the dogs had filled a void I hadn't truly recognized. I found myself clearing up after Buster, who pulled his toys out of the basket we kept them in, and when he prodded me awake in the morning, I was transported back to when Derek and David were little and would rush into our room on a Sunday morning, desperate for us to get up and play.

Tragedy struck just before Christmas when, one morning, Venger couldn't get up. We took him to the vet, and this time, there were no pills to help him. We told him we loved him and the vet put him to sleep. I thought my heart would break in two.

When we arrived home, Buster rushed to me, circled around me, then stared at the door. *Where's my friend?*

I knelt down and told him, in words he couldn't possibly understand: 'Venger's gone, my darling.' I petted him and stroked him, then held him close because I reckoned that was a language Buster would understand. He stayed in my arms for a while, not getting bored or wanting his toys. He sensed that Terry and I needed him and stayed by our sides. He was such a comfort to have around.

We decided to downsize from our large family home. The house was simply too big for us, the garden too much work. We found a lovely new home with more than enough room for the three of us and our offer was accepted. As the process got under way, Terry and I had the mammoth task of packing up a lifetime of belongings. It was bittersweet when we found the odd children's book in the loft, a remnant of the family we'd nurtured together, but we were excited, too, about the move.

Months later, Buster's prostate cancer returned. There was no treatment that would hold it at bay as it was too advanced. Once more, Terry and I went to the vet and left without the dog we'd come to love so much. This time when we got home the silence was deafening. With Buster gone, who would comfort us now? The dogs had given our days structure, colour and light, and the loss of their companionship was a bitter pill to swallow.

The grief gripped me at the oddest times. I'd be working my way through a pile of ironing while Terry ran an errand or did some shopping and I'd look up from my ironing table, expecting Venger or Buster to be snoozing nearby or watching me. Instead I'd see an empty space and hear only the hissing of the steam iron.

Those were the moments when it hit me: I felt empty without a dog.

My instinct was to get another dog to fill that void but something held me back.

I'd read a book that said it was not good to get a new dog while you were grieving for one that had gone. The author had explained that if you're grieving you'll go into the new relationship with sadness. During that time, the new dog will pick up on your emotions and feel sorry for you. I didn't want that to be the case but I couldn't stifle my longing, and that was when Terry and I found ourselves at Battersea Dogs & Cats Home. We registered our details and later walked slowly along the kennels, looking at every dog and reading each profile. We knew we wanted another dog, but which one would be the right match?

Right at the end of our tour, I noticed a dog sitting quietly in her kennel. She was a beautiful Ridgeback cross, and when I arrived in front of her, something wonderful happened. Tammy looked at me with such love and recognition that she might have been saying hello to me for the hundredth time, not the first. I looked at her and she gazed at me. In that moment, we fell in love.

Tammy came home with us that day, and for the first time in our lives, we had a daughter. Terry adored her as much as I did and we took her for long walks in the morning and evening. Whenever we went on holiday we made sure it was to a hotel or B&B in the UK that accepted canine guests. We didn't spend a day apart.

She was mostly quite a noisy presence but some days the house would fall silent and I'd find Tammy hiding under our bed. We didn't know what had happened in her past, but I could feel the insecurity rolling off her in waves. I'd kneel down and say, 'Come on, girl, come out, you're OK.' She'd edge her way forward for a cuddle. Sometimes I'd worry that the grief she'd felt in me when she'd first arrived in our home had caused her to feel she couldn't come to me for comfort when she needed it, which made me sad. But I knew the only way forward was to find her every time she hid and give her the comfort she might have felt unable to ask for.

Other times, we'd be out and she'd suddenly cower behind me, but I realized there was a pattern to that: she did it whenever she saw a man in a cap or a hat. Again I wondered about her life before us. What had happened to cause her to react like that? Sometimes I'd look into her soulful eyes and will her to tell me. I knew it wasn't possible, of course, but it didn't stop me wondering.

Luckily, I worked only four hours a day, when our lovely neighbour would take Tammy into his home. I'd return to find her staring at me from next door's living-room window. The look of anticipation in her eyes warmed my heart.

We made some changes for Tammy's sake. We swapped our Honda 4x4 for a Subaru that was closer to the ground so she could get in and out of the back with ease.

Eventually, she developed skin cancer on her chest. We nursed her until we knew that no amount of treatment or medication would make her better. When Tammy was thirteen, two years after her diagnosis, she became disoriented and couldn't walk. She was shaking her head constantly, and the vet reckoned the cancer had spread: she had a tumour in her ear, affecting her balance and co-ordination. With heavy hearts, we knew it was Tammy's time. In mid-November as the frost set in, we took her to the vet and stayed with her till her eyes closed and her chest stilled.

When we got home, there was no furry face to greet us, and our home, though smaller than the family one we'd spent years in, felt suddenly like a cavernous, echoing space. Despite the pictures of our family on the walls, and all our belongings, which made the house our home, it was as if the soul of the place had been sucked out. I worried that some of my friends who didn't have dogs wouldn't understand how sad I was about Tammy and didn't talk to them about it. How could I explain to them that the grief I felt for Tammy was similar to that which I'd felt when I'd lost my parents? It seemed silly to say it out loud, but that was how I felt. Nothing brought me happiness, and I could see Terry felt the same.

We had her cremated and when we received her ashes, I cried and cried. But it gave me comfort to have her in our house again, in whatever form.

By now Terry and I had retired and this was the perfect time to do some travelling. For years, we'd dreamt of going back to Australia where we'd lived for eight years and where our children were born. Yet we couldn't bring ourselves to look at any travel brochures or flight costs. Our life had involved so many changes in recent years – retirement, a new home and the loss of Tammy – that maybe a trip away and a new adventure was exactly what we needed.

The more we talked about it, though, the more we

realized that no place we went to would mean anything to us without a dog, which left us wondering something: was it right to bring a dog into our lives now?

Two weeks after we'd lost Tammy, we came to a conclusion. We could splash out on an amazing holiday for two or three weeks, but when we returned to our home in Surrey, we'd still be unhappy. Nothing would bring us as much pleasure as a dog.

'It's more important that we're happy day to day,' I told Terry.

'I completely agree. Let's take a trip to Battersea tomorrow.'

We visited Battersea Old Windsor and looked around the kennels but, sadly, none of the dogs grabbed our attention.

On our way out, a member of the public pulled up in a van. When he got out, he opened the passenger door and took out an open box. Immediately the air was filled with the whines and yelps of tiny puppies.

I stopped him. 'May I have a look?'

'Of course.'

Inside the box seven tiny brindle puppies were wriggling and writhing over each other. They were beautiful – had I seen them inside, I would have been taking one home with me. But it would be a while before those Staffie pups were ready for rehoming, and I didn't think I could wait.

On the train journey home Terry and I agreed that none of the dogs we'd seen had felt right for us. For me, picking a dog is like picking a new friend. You can meet a person you like but it can be some time before you find another that you like just as much. Would I ever love another dog as I'd loved Tammy?

We arrived home feeling blue. Tammy had been a real daddy's girl and Terry missed her just as much as I did. He didn't have to say it but I knew what he was likely to be thinking. Maybe it wasn't meant for us to have another dog. But I was ever the optimist and I hoped there was something very special in store for us.

Christmas that year came and went quietly. Terry and I were not in the mood and didn't put up a tree or swap presents. Instead, we went to our son Derek and his wife Katie's home in Northamptonshire for a quiet family day with our grandchildren. Katie always put on a beautiful Christmas, and that year was no exception. Her home twinkled with fairy lights and she cooked the most amazing dinner.

Underneath, though, Tammy's absence weighed heavily upon us. Had it not been for our prearranged plans, Terry and I would have stayed at home because we were having a difficult time coming to terms with Tammy's death. It was hard for us to celebrate anything without her.

Five days later, Terry and I decided to try Battersea in London. It was quite busy but a rehomer, Sarah, was able to talk us through the procedures and ask us what we had in mind. As we were previous owners, who'd taken a dog home from Battersea, our details were still on the system so she invited us to have a look around the kennels. 'Let me know if you see any dogs you'd like to meet,' she said.

Terry and I were looking for a dog around two years old, which didn't need to be trained like a puppy but would be with us for a considerable time. We couldn't take the grief of another loss so soon, should we take in an older dog.

Sarah showed us to a meeting room, then went to fetch a young Staffie we'd seen earlier and pointed out to her. She brought her back for us and, after a gentle introduction, left us to get to know her.

She was very playful, and even when we put the ball away, she went looking for it. But we could see she was more interested in her ball than getting to know us and was not the social dog we wanted. She wasn't the one who would bring us the companionship we were missing but we were certain she'd be great for a family with children looking for a fun dog with play in mind.

Now it was late in the afternoon and I was losing hope that we'd find a dog that day.

When Sarah returned, we shared our thoughts and a frown of concentration crossed her face. After a few moments, she said: 'Would you be interested in a puppy?'

I looked at Terry with a never-say-never expression. 'We'll have a look,' he said.

Sarah smiled. 'I'll go and get him so you can meet him.'

Minutes later, she returned and in her arms was a

beautiful blond puppy with a grey face and ears. I couldn't help but gasp. 'He's gorgeous!' I said.

Sarah nodded and placed the puppy on the floor. 'This is Dancer. His litter arrived here shortly before Christmas Eve, and we named them all after Father Christmas's reindeer.'

I thought it was a perfect name for him as he danced about excitedly by our feet, stopping for strokes as he brushed past us. We learnt that he was an Akita cross and likely to be a decent size. He was only a foot high right now, but even if he did become quite big, I knew it wouldn't be a problem: we'd handled a large dog and could do it again.

I glanced at Terry and, to my delight, his face was lit up, much like mine must have been. I thought: *Yes! This little puppy is the one!*

'He's a real sweetie,' Sarah told us.

That much was clear. We sat on the floor while Dancer sniffed us and everything else in the room. He wasn't timid, frightened or needy. He was, in fact, a little bit cocky and, as he bounded over my lap and into Terry's, I loved him instantly.

We told Sarah we'd love to be Dancer's new family.

Dancer and his litter had come in suffering with giardiasis, a parasitic infection in the intestine, and Sarah wanted the vet to have a chat with us about it.

When he arrived, he said: 'We're quite positive Dancer will be OK, but we'd like to keep him here for a couple more days, just to keep an eye on him.' We were desperate to take Dancer home but what the vet was saying was for the best: giardiasis can be fatal in puppies, if it goes unchecked. And while the wait would be agonising, it meant we had a bit of time to prepare the house for Dancer's arrival.

We returned home on the train, but this time, instead of feeling sad, we were elated.

We had plans with our neighbours that night, and when we arrived for drinks, Terry took out his phone and showed everybody a picture of Dancer. 'That's our new puppy,' he said.

'Isn't he gorgeous?' I added.

We couldn't stop talking about him and our friends couldn't wait to meet Dancer – we had decided to rename him Sam.

On the Internet we learnt what we could about what to expect from an Akita, and on New Year's Eve, we bought bedding, toys, food and a cage, if he wanted it, to help Sam feel secure and safe in the house. We saw in the New Year full of excitement and were jittery with the anticipation of picking Sam up and bringing him home. The next day, we did just that, armed with leaflets and a book from Battersea about how to care for a puppy.

On the way Sam was ill in the car. I put it down to nerves and excitement.

We got him home and, like a child at bathtime, Sam stood in the tub and let me wash him. As I rinsed his soft fur with warm water, he looked at me and wagged his tail. His eyes were telling me: *Thank you, Mummy.*

The only time he moved was to try to bite the flow of water pouring over him. It was so adorable I wanted to squeeze his gorgeous little face.

It had been many years since I'd bathed a child and never a puppy but it felt familiar to me and I cherished that lovely moment between us.

But the following day Sam was hot, feverish and lethargic. He became floppy and I called Battersea, who advised me to bring him back to be checked over in the clinic.

I was worried it might be the giardiasis, so Terry and I rushed him straight to London.

At Battersea's clinic the vet took Sam's temperature, which was high.

'What does that mean?' I asked anxiously.

He said Sam needed to be put on a drip as he was showing signs of dehydration.

'How long will that take?' I asked.

'I'm afraid he'll have to stay here overnight.'

My stomach dropped, the way it does when you drive up a hill and dip down over the other side. Three times in my life I'd gone into a veterinary clinic with a dog I loved and left without them. Would this time end in tragedy too?

I couldn't bear the thought.

I couldn't bring myself to say goodbye to Sam so I left with a new, stubborn thought in mind: I'd be back to pick up our puppy. And soon.

I spent the night in bits and barely slept for worry.

But I knew that Sam was in safe hands at the Battersea clinic and told myself so every time my stomach rolled in that horrible, anxious way.

Early the next morning, I phoned for an update.

'Sam perked up after being on the drip,' the nurse said. 'His temperature has gone down . . .'

There was a pause and my heart skipped a beat.

Then she said: 'He's quite mischievous, isn't he?'

I was so relieved. 'He can be as mischievous as he wants,' I replied, trying hard not to cry, 'as long as we can bring him home.'

She told me Sam was ready to be picked up so, once more, we drove into London to collect him.

When he was brought out, he leapt into my arms and I didn't let him go.

On our way out, the nurse gave us a tip. 'My dog is clever and mischievous like Sam and I play a little game with him that he loves. Maybe Sam will like it too.'

When she explained what it was, I said: 'We'll have to give it a try.'

Back home, I placed a treat on the table and, with Sam on my lap, I covered the treat with an upturned melamine breakfast bowl. I placed two empty bowls next to the one with a treat in it and, like a magician, whizzed the bowls this way and that.

When all the whizzing had come to a stop, Sam reached out and tapped the bowl on the right with his paw.

I lifted it up and there was the treat. 'What a clever little boy you are, Sam!'

From then on, that was Sam's favourite game. But after a while I discovered I could do it without the treat and Sam was still happy. As long as he got his paws on that bowl, he was chuffed.

I replaced the melamine bowls with stainless-steel ones, and the minute Sam got hold of one, he was off around our home. He pushed it this way and that way and flipped it over. Whenever he got too excited and shoved it under the sofa by mistake, he came looking for me or Terry and whined at us until we followed him to where he'd lost the bowl. We started taking it in turns – it happened so often.

Just like the nurse at Battersea had told us, Sam was indeed mischievous. If I was wearing a dressing-gown and the cord from the waist was hanging down, Sam would be jumping up at me and grabbing it. If I left a slipper unsupervised or if Terry kicked off his socks, Sam was straight on to them. It was like having a tiny child in the house and thoroughly lovely.

It made me think back to the days when Derek and David had started toddling around and talking to us in the baby chatter that makes your heart melt.

The yawning emptiness we'd felt after losing Tammy was a distant memory. Now our life was entirely filled with Sam. Our home felt alive with fun and colour, his toys in every room. Sometimes he slept in the cage we'd set up in the kitchen, but mostly he liked his special spot in our bedroom. He'd wait on our bed as Terry and I brushed our teeth, and when we came in, he'd try his luck.

Terry and I would manoeuvre ourselves under the covers and if Sam hadn't gone to his little spot between the wardrobe and my bedside table, I'd say: 'Sam, are you going to get into your own bed?'

He would play dumb for a couple of minutes but we knew that he was very smart.

The moment I said, 'If you don't get into your own bed, Sam, you'll have to sleep in the kitchen,' he would move. It did the trick every time. Again, he reminded me of when our children were young and they'd sneak into our bed after a nightmare or just for a cuddle.

Throughout the winter, Terry got up in the middle of the night to let Sam out for a wee, and I'd hold back my laughter as he pulled on trousers over his pyjama bottoms, then a jumper and coat. We both knew Sam wouldn't be in a hurry to come back inside. He wasn't a big fan of snow and didn't like it if the ground was wet, but he could be quite stubborn, typical of his Akita background. If he didn't want to come in, he would sit on the pavement and refuse to budge. When they finally returned, Sam would snuggle under Terry's neck in the bed and we'd let him get away with that one. But as Sam grew and threatened to shove me out of bed, I'd tell him: 'If you don't move over, Sam, you'll have to go in your own bed.'

That was enough and he'd straighten himself out.

When spring arrived, we decided to take Sam to puppy class to ensure he was trained properly. He rubbed along well with the other dogs, but at the end of each session, when the dogs were allowed a little play as a treat, Sam seemed always to be the one in trouble. The lady who provided the training told me Sam was a bit of a bully, which worried me.

I called Battersea to speak to one of the behaviour-ists about my concerns and was put in touch with a lady who trained dogs for TV programmes. She came along to meet Sam at home. I told her my worries, then said, 'If there's a problem with Sam's behaviour, I'd like to nip it in the bud.'

'I understand, but let's have a look at how he inter-acts with other dogs first.'

We all set off to the park and there we let Sam and her dog, a beautiful Collie, off their leads to have a play. They ran circles around each other and dashed about together just fine.

'He's doing exactly what I'd expect him to do,' the trainer said. 'Sam will be absolutely fine. Just keep doing what you're doing.'

It was such a relief to know we were doing the right thing by Sam and I was so happy I'd made that call to Battersea.

We did some extra training sessions with Sam after the first course and took him on lots of day trips. From our home in Surrey, we ventured to various parks and National Trust sites and he got on well with every dog he encountered. The worries I'd had about his behav-iour melted away as he proved himself over and over. Sam was very well behaved and so handsome that everywhere we went people stopped us to talk about him. I was so proud of him. Terry and I told them about his Christmas arrival at Battersea and how we'd taken him on. I told everyone we met: 'He's changed our lives.'

And he really had. We found ourselves getting up at seven to take him for his morning walk. We met so many new people and got chatting to other dog owners while we were out and about. When I described him to Rita, one of the ladies I walked with, she said: 'Wasn't he in the newspaper at Christmas?'

I didn't know anything about that.

'There was something in the *Daily Mail* about a gorgeous litter of Akita cross puppies who needed a new home on Christmas Day,' Rita went on. 'One of them had a grey face – it must have been Sam!'

When I got home, I turned the computer on and, with Terry at my side, Googled for the article. A link appeared: 'Santa's little yelpers'.

We clicked into it and there on the screen were eight gorgeous little puppies, including Sam. That made me think about Sam's brothers and sisters. Where had they ended up?

I sent a picture of Sam to Battersea's magazine *Paws* and it was published. In time, two families who had adopted Sam's brothers, Cupid and Prancer, contacted the magazine too. One had paid for a DNA test, which showed the puppies are an Akita, Foxhound and Staffie mix.

It felt good to know more about Sam, and now we knew the mix, it was easy to attribute his traits to his heritage. Whenever he had a soft, gentle moment, his

Staffie background shone through. When we were at home and somebody knocked, he rushed to the door to check out our visitor – typical of the loyal, protective behaviour Akitas are known for. As for his Foxhound genes, we reckoned they fuelled his adventurous side.

On walks, Sam would make a beeline for the patisserie near our home. We knew what he wanted so we'd stop for a coffee and a croissant and treat Sam to a nibble. After a while, he came to understand that he'd get his proper breakfast after we'd walked him, so in the mornings, he'd refuse to leave the house until we'd fed him.

He was too clever for his own good and ours!

Every day at four o'clock, it wasn't Sam's tummy rumbling that caught my attention, it was his chatter. He'd come to me and urge me into the kitchen. Once he got me there, he stared at the drawer that he knew his dinner was kept in. If I didn't do as he asked, or I forgot to give him a treat, he'd bark at me.

To keep Sam stimulated, we took him to doggy daycare once a week where he had a chance to run around with lots of other dogs. He absolutely loved it, and whenever we got into the car and turned into a certain road, he'd start howling and whining in anticipation of arriving at his favourite place. It was fun for Sam but also good for Terry and me to have an afternoon getting odd jobs done or seeing friends.

Other than those days, Sam came everywhere with us, just like Tammy had before him, and Venger and Buster before her. We took walking holidays around the coast or to Gloucestershire and the Cotswolds. He loved to wallow in the mud pools left behind by tractors and we let him get on with it. Afterwards, he'd stand perfectly still and let us wash him down with a bowl of water, no fuss.

As the year went on, Terry and I decided to sell our home and move to a beautiful converted farmhouse on the West Sussex coast. There, we'd have a duplex apartment with a garden for Sam and walks in the nearby countryside. Everything was set for us to enjoy our first Christmas in our new home so I bought a brand-new tree and decorations and packed it all away, ready to put up after the move. I made a food order online, to arrive at our new home on Christmas Eve.

Our old home was filled with boxes, forty-one in the living room, when, just days before the move to the South Downs, our buyer dropped out. It was such a blow but, instead of feeling sad, I pulled out the Christmas tree and set it up in the living room between piles of boxes. It was all because of Sam that I found the will to do it. Having him with us had filled us with excitement for Christmas and I was not about to let the move falling through ruin it.

On Christmas Day, we woke up early, surrounded by boxes and the gorgeous Christmas tree, and swapped presents. The only thing Terry and I were really interested in was seeing Sam open his. He loved ripping off the wrapping paper, and when he discovered he had a new ball, it became his pride and joy for the rest of the day.

Later, Terry and I went to the pub across the road with our neighbours who, like us, had family living far away. Sam was with us in the bar for most of the day. In a quiet moment, I nudged Terry. 'Isn't this a world away from last year?'

He nodded, knowing I was thinking about Tammy. 'How life moves on . . .' he said wistfully.

Now, Sam is three years old, and doesn't realize how big he is. Every morning he jumps on the bed, like he did when he was a puppy, and lies on top of me, covering me from head to toe, as if he's as light as a feather. He has his mad minutes but he's a good boy and will do as he's told. He's like a teenager, in some respects, growing into the sweetest dog, coming into his own, learning new things and understanding more about the world. Like Derek and David in that phase, Sam is forming his own relationships. If we skip a party with our neighbours and take Sam out, it's only an hour or two before our phones start beeping. *Where's Sam? Won't you bring him over? We miss him . . .*

I feel like a proud parent because, in a lot of ways, having a dog is like having a child. Emotionally, you go through similar things. He's as soft as he looks and makes Terry and me very happy because of the companionship he offers. He also gets us out and about. For a retired couple like us, it's not just about having a dog: we're adopting a certain lifestyle and that's what we adore about having a dog like Sam.

Nothing can bring us more joy, love and company than a dog and Sam ticks all of those boxes for us. He's brought us back from a very unhappy place and has made us feel fulfilled and content with our lot in life.

Without Battersea, none of this would have been possible. It took us three visits to their centres before we found Sam, but the rehomers worked with us to make sure we were matched correctly.

I won't ever understand how any owner could love and nurture a dog for years, then give them up but I'm grateful that a place like Battersea exists. Because of Battersea, people like us, who are in a position to offer an animal unconditional love, can take in a dog who will give back all that love and care.

And you can't put a price on it.

8. A Twist of Fate

The Charmer

Making my early-morning rounds of Battersea's kennels, I came across a little white scruff of a dog. From the description on his kennel, I could see he was a Jack Russell cross and only four months old. Looking into his sad puppy-dog eyes, I felt a funny warm feeling spread out from my chest, down my arms and into my fingertips. I just knew Charlie was going to be my dog.

I was head of Intake and Assessment at Battersea Dogs & Cats Home. Over the three years I'd spent working there, I'd seen hundreds of animals come and go, and every now and then, one would capture my heart. For months, I'd been thinking of looking for a feisty, hard-working Patterdale Terrier but now, seeing Charlie shaking and looking a bit sorry for himself, I was certain he belonged with me.

I introduced myself. Then he looked up at me with eyes that said, *Get me out of here, Liz,* and I was smitten.

Charlie had come in days earlier as a stray. He'd been found tied up near London City Airport, with a small empty food bowl beside him. Whoever had abandoned him had felt some responsibility towards him, but how anyone could abandon a puppy like that was beyond me. Luckily for Charlie, a passer-by had found him and kept him for a week before handing him in to us for rehoming.

I wanted to be the one who gave Charlie a new home but there was a problem. He was already earmarked as a possible working dog in our service dogs programme, which finds working homes for some of our animals with the right temperament to cope in such environments. They may become sniffer dogs and search for drugs, people, arms, cigarettes and cash. Charlie, however, seemed suitable for a trainer who worked with dogs in TV and film. It wasn't ideal, given that I wanted him, but I took it on the chin. It was just one of those things. As he was a puppy, I volunteered to foster him at home until his seven 'stray days' were up, and he was officially the Home's property, legally available for rehoming.

That night, Charlie came home to my flat and was no longer the shaky, nervous little dog I'd seen in the kennel. He was cocky, confident and strutted around like he owned the place.

It was impossible not to fall in love with his brattish personality, even if he was a handful at times. He was a lovable rogue with a bit of attitude, but I liked that. I took Charlie to work with me, and at the station he had a habit of finding food, a discarded chicken wing or some gum, to gobble up. He had the uncanny ability to spot something he considered edible at a hundred paces, and once he had it in his jaws, it was near impossible to get it out, so fast could he swallow it.

I resorted to using a harness that muzzled his mouth, not because he was aggressive but because it gave me a fighting chance to wrangle away from him whatever rubbish he'd found on the floor!

As I got to know Charlie, I wondered why the passer-by who'd found him at the airport had brought him to Battersea instead of keeping him. I reckoned it was because of his naughty streak. I could see that if Charlie didn't go to a working home, and was rehomed to a family, it wasn't out of the realm of possibility that he would be given back to Battersea because of his mischievous ways. However, if his new owner had experience of terriers, and understood Charlie's rebellious streak, they might be happy to put up with it. Someone like me, who found it endearing. But anyone who hadn't had a dog before, and was sucked in by Charlie's adorable, deceptively innocent face, would be in for a shock. These were the scenarios that came to mind in the time he spent with me, and I wished there was a way I could take him on, but I had to leave that one up to Fate.

During the week that I fostered Charlie, I took him for a walk at lunchtime in Battersea Park. He was full of himself and raced around with delight at being outside.

When his stray days were up, I had some good news.

The rehoming team had found the TV trainer another suitable dog and Charlie was up for adoption once more. I went to straight to the office and signed the paperwork to make him officially mine.

I soon discovered that Charlie had a fiery temperament, which he displayed mostly over resources. If he had a tennis ball or another toy, he gave you a look that warned: *I dare you to take it off me.* He was quite fussy with people too. He rarely liked them but that didn't stop him playing with their emotions. On our commute to work, he'd wag his tail and stare at other passengers with those appealing eyes. As soon as somebody stooped to say hello, he'd turn up his nose at them and trot away. He loved nothing more than enticing people to pay attention to him, then flat-out rejecting their advances. I spent half my time out with him apologizing and explaining away his behaviour, telling his victims: 'Sorry, he's a bit moody sometimes.' I couldn't very well say that this apparently adorable little dog was terribly manipulative.

He settled into the office quite well and would find a chair or a corner to snooze in. Between our trips to and from work, and his lunchtime run, he was quite relaxed. That didn't stop him trampling across my desk, sitting on my keyboard and firing off random gobbledegook emails with his bum. Whenever I got up, I told him: 'Don't you steal my chair now, will you, Charlie?' Not that it did any good. As soon as I was out of sight, I heard the patter of his feet bounding across the office and jumping into my seat.

He must have known when I was coming back, by smell or sound, because as I neared my office, I'd hear the chair spinning as Charlie jumped off and ran back to his own spot. I often asked him, 'If this is what you're like with paws, what would you get up to if you had opposable thumbs?'

He didn't need to answer because I already knew. He loved outsmarting people and dogs and felt no need of friendship beyond mine. I was secretly chuffed I was the only one with that privilege.

He tolerated other dogs and loved nothing more than winding them up. Unluckily for most of the canines with which he came into contact, Charlie was smarter than they were. It became a constant source of amusement to watch him figure out ways to get the better of his peers.

When my flatmate brought a Staffie home, Charlie took it upon himself to show him the ropes. He ran around the coffee-table with a toy, tempting the Staffie into a chase. Round and round they went until the Staffie was hot on Charlie's heels. Then Charlie slid underneath the table and out the other side, leaving the other dog baffled.

After a while I recognized I could put his wily ways to good use. When new dogs came in to the Home and needed to be tested for temperament – say, former racing dogs like Greyhounds and Lurchers – Charlie was great at playing the stooge. I made sure the two dogs were separated by a wire fence, then set Charlie off on a run to test the other dog's chase instinct. It helped us figure out if that instinct would pose a problem for their new owner and to advise them properly.

Other times, I would simply take Charlie to the fence with a newbie waiting on the other side, then observe his behaviour. As he was usually cocky, it was a warning sign if he backed away. That told me to keep an eye out: the other dog was exuding a certain something that us humans couldn't pick up on.

As Charlie settled in at the office and at home, his true colours began to show.

By day, he conserved his energy between walks, but the minute we got home, he'd have a five-minute mad dash about the place, which I called his Whirling Dervish, then slump on the sofa with me for the rest of the evening. By nightfall, though, I was convinced Charlie had plans. He often stalked about the flat at dead of night, and I began to imagine what life for Charlie was like when he was out of earshot. I reckoned he had a secret plot for world domination and had developed it at an early age. When people picked up on how wily he was, I told them, 'I bet his first word to his mother was an expletive.' When they got to know him better, they'd understand what I'd meant.

In time, it became clear that Charlie would remain physically small, but also that he had a big brain and an even bigger attitude. Charlie could sniff out tennis balls that were seemingly miles away and would power through hedges to get to them. Nothing was too much of a challenge for him and he tackled everything head-on. But how had he worked his way into my heart and home? He had an uncanny ability to ooze charm and make friends wherever he went. Over time, the regulars on our commute saved Charlie a seat while I was left to stand. As he was usually nonplussed by them, or had once rejected their advances, they would get into a stir if Charlie climbed on to their lap. They'd stare at him in wonder and then, while having a tentative stroke, they'd turn to me and say, 'Gosh, look at that! He must like me after all.'

Charlie would glance at me with a twinkle in his eye and I'd know what he was really up to. I didn't have the heart to tell them Charlie was only after one thing: a good nose out of the window. So they continued loving Charlie, and even invited him to summer barbecues and birthday parties. At Christmas, the fan club Charlie had gathered for himself showered him with gift-wrapped treats, stockings and even festive cards! Of course, I didn't receive a thing. And while Charlie sat there among his friends, surrounded by goodies, I thought, *You little user!* But all the qualities wrapped up in that mad little dog made me love him dearly.

When he wanted to be charming, nobody was immune to his ways. Lucky for him, Charlie had one of those faces that made people grab hold of him so cuddles were never in short supply.

But I learnt to read Charlie's moods. If he rolled on to his back, looking submissive and cute as a button, I'd warn people: 'Don't get sucked in. He wants to look cute for you but he's not after a cuddle.' In the office, when he was on his favourite chair, we all knew better than to try to move him. He often looked as if he was desperate for a tickle but would snap at you before he let you touch him. It was all part and parcel of his game plan.

I reckoned Charlie had stashed a cache of weapons, blueprints and ammunition in some safe place for when he launched his one-dog offensive to take over the world. He was always up to something and had some pretty funny delusions of grandeur. Whenever he caught sight of his reflection, he puffed out his chest. I bet he didn't see his cute fluffy mug staring back: all Charlie would see was the massive Rottweiler he imagined he was.

It certainly explained the confusion that crossed his face when I scooped him up and carried him somewhere. He'd look down at the air beneath his feet and then to me as if to say: *How are you doing this? You must be SO strong!*

He was a little rascal, but I loved him and his quirky personality to bits. I was as attached to him as he was to me, and on our days off from work, I treated him to long walks around Crystal Palace and the park near our home in Penge, south-east London.

One Saturday, the sun was shining and it was a perfect day for Charlie to chase squirrels and generally cause a bit of mischief. I grabbed his lead. 'Park, Charlie. Let's go.'

When we got there, we set off along one of the winding paths and passed a bin. Something made me grind to a halt – much to Charlie's dismay. I could have sworn I'd heard a rustling noise. I waited to hear it again, and just when I was about to give up and carry on with our walk, there it was. This time, Charlie heard it too. It was indeed coming from the big bin to the left of us. It wasn't an open-top bin, but when Charlie circled around it and showed an interest, I tried to peer inside one of the four slot-like gaps on the side. As the rustling continued, I spotted the pointy, gingery ears of what appeared to be a fox. From its size, I reckoned it was a cub.

Just then, a lady with a Labrador stopped next to me. She must have thought I looked like a lunatic, so I said, 'There's an animal in this bin.'

When her dog showed an interest too, I knew I hadn't imagined those ears, and when some passers-by wanted to put some rubbish into the bin, I had to stop them.

'There's an animal in there,' I told them. 'Please use the next one along.'

By now, a small group had gathered around us and we tried to figure out what to do. As the minutes ticked by, I realized the animal was unlikely to be a fox. Whatever was in there had been forced through the slot by a human. No animal of that size – wild or otherwise – could have jumped up and got into the bin at that odd angle. *It's got to be a puppy in there,* I thought.

I put Charlie back on his lead – he had a face like thunder at his walk being interrupted before it had even begun – and told the group to keep watch while I went back down the hill to the ranger's office.

'It's probably a squirrel,' he said. 'Maybe you should just leave it alone.'

I said: 'OK, it's a squirrel . . . if you think squirrels have massive orange pointy ears!'

That got his attention.

I walked Charlie back to the bin and the ranger arrived moments later in his Land Rover. The bins in the park had all been emptied the day before and the lids were locked shut. The ranger had what seemed like a million keys on his chain but none of them fitted. In the end, he ripped the lid off with his bare hands.

Finally, I could have a good look at the animal.

There, sitting in the middle of a heap of empty crisps packets, tissues and bottles, was a beautiful red-headed animal. Whether he was a fox cub or a puppy, there was only one way to find out. I reached in and pulled him into my arms. He was beautifully calm and friendly and I felt sure then that he wasn't a fox cub. By nature, a fox would have been snapping at me and desperate to get away. This little guy was perfectly content to be handled and cuddled.

As the realization spread that he was indeed a puppy, bystanders offered there and then to give him a home. I told them I worked at Battersea and was going to take him there, where I knew he would be in the best possible hands.

As we made our way back to the car, Charlie was fed up. He didn't like puppies and now his walk was ruined.

The three of us went back to my flat and I set the puppy, which I'd nicknamed Pete from Penge, on the carpet. After a sniff around, he tried to play with Charlie. Charlie came to me and nudged me. *Make him go away*, he pleaded with his eyes.

While Pete had a run around my flat, I arranged for a colleague, who lived downstairs, to lend me a cat cage so I could transport Pete to Battersea safely. It was just the right size for the little fella. He got into it willingly and I placed him in my car. Charlie jumped into the passenger seat, staunchly facing forwards.

He might have lost a walk that afternoon but I wound the window down, and as we drove along with Charlie enjoying the warm breeze, it was clear that my dog was almost ready to forgive me.

I'd called ahead and given the Battersea team a heads-up, and when I arrived, they were discussing Pete's likely breed. Eventually the vet agreed with me that Pete couldn't possibly be a fox. He was definitely a puppy, despite his foxy colour and distinctive ears, probably a terrier cross, between eight and ten weeks old. As he was in pretty good shape, he was taken to the puppy area of the kennels to keep him away from infection. Battersea is home to around four hundred dogs at any one time, so the risk of infections, like kennel cough, or conditions such as parvovirus, is taken very seriously. They can be deadly, and puppies are especially vulnerable to picking them up.

Pete was quickly sent out to be fostered, much like my Charlie had been, because of his young age. We didn't know anything about his background but he could not have got into that bin himself. Somebody had posted him, like a bit of rubbish, through the lid. Had he not been found, he would have died of dehydration and starvation because he couldn't have made his own way out.

After seven days at Battersea, when nobody had claimed him, we were ready to start the rehoming process. Three people had shown an interest in him, but it was when the team met Gemma that they knew they had the right match . . .

A New Play Pal

As we unpacked the last box, my husband Dave and I slumped on the sofa. Across the living room in our new house, Ted, our seven-year-old rescue Border Terrier, picked a spot and flopped down too. We had spent a sweltering July day moving from our old place into this, our family home, and we were all exhausted. Now that everything had been unpacked, I realized all the effort had been worthwhile. The rooms upstairs and down were bigger than they had been in our old house, and we had an extra bedroom. We also had five acres of land: perfect for what we had in mind.

Dave and I had always said that when we'd settled into a big family home we'd get another dog to keep Ted company. We'd lived with Dave's parents for eighteen months, and Ted had loved having a friend in their

Labrador, Willow. We wanted him to have a companion. As we were thinking of starting a family soon, we reckoned a puppy would be best. We were happy to have another rescue dog, but without knowing the dog's full history, I felt more comfortable with a puppy. Taking on a young dog, I'd have more control over how its behaviour developed.

We set about renovating our house, and a year later, it was finally ready for our much-wanted new arrivals. I looked around the local rescue centre but without success. It was disappointing and I felt a bit disheartened. Then I learnt something that gave me an incentive to concentrate on the search: I was pregnant. If we wanted another dog before the baby arrived, we had to get a move on. We'd taken Ted, who was initially a bit aggressive, from Battersea Dogs & Cats Home – we'd been good candidates for the job as I was a veterinary nurse and Dave a vet. Afterwards, we'd stayed in touch with some of the staff at the Home, and while the ones we'd made friends with had gone to new jobs, some had stayed in touch with their former colleagues.

That was how I came to learn of a little puppy called Pete.

I gave Battersea a call and chatted to a rehomer. We talked about what I was after. I didn't mention Pete straight away and hoped the lady would use her matching skills to tally him with us. If she did, it would be a sign that he was right for us.

She said: 'Gemma, we have a puppy here at the moment and he's not doing very well in the kennels.

163

One of our girls has been taking him home after work every night as a foster but he really needs a home.' He was a Terrier cross named Pete.

I knew it.

Next day, Dave and I took Ted to Battersea. We were shown to a big meeting room upstairs while one of the staff nipped off to fetch Pete. When she returned, her colleague Helen came in too. They set Pete down. The little chap was adorable: he had pointy ears, fluffy red fur and a face you wanted to kiss. He and Ted said a quick and unremarkable hello to each other, and before Dave and I could introduce ourselves to him, Pete was off sniffing all the nooks and crannies of the room.

Helen stepped forward. 'I've been fostering Pete so I thought I'd come and tell you a bit about what I've learnt.'

'That would be great,' Dave and I said in unison.

Helen smiled. 'He's been getting on well with my cat so he shouldn't have a problem with other animals.'

That was a relief: we already had a cat at home.

'But you may need to keep an eye on him for a little while as he definitely has that small-dog attitude. Watch out for bad behaviour that you need to nip in the bud.'

As Helen told us what she had learnt about Pete, I felt the muscles in my shoulders relax and took a deep breath. Background information on a stray or a rescue dog was usually thin on the ground, so it was valuable to have Helen on hand to give us a profile of Pete from what she'd observed, and tell of his experience. That expert advice was why we'd come to Battersea. When we'd picked up Ted years earlier, they'd gone the extra mile to give us as much information and guidance on him as possible. Battersea had stood out for us then and I knew now that we'd made the right choice in coming to the Home again.

I listened to all the information Helen gave us, then said: 'I have one reservation. Pete is a bit on the small side and we have lots of land so I'm worried he might escape through one of the perimeter fences.' I also told Helen and her colleague that we kept sheep on our land and asked their opinion. Their answers reassured me.

Helen explained: 'He's still very young and he's already the size of a Chihuahua so hopefully he'll be too big when he's fully grown to slip through your fence.'

I knew then that I wanted Pete whether he was small or not.

We put Ted and Pete on their leads and took them for a walk. They didn't pay much attention to each other and walked well together. It wasn't the sparks and fireworks I was hoping for at the start of their friendship but I told Dave: 'It's better than them not getting on, I suppose!'

Dave smiled. 'Yes, it could be worse. Maybe it'll just take a bit of time.'

I thought back to our time at Dave's parents' home: it had taken Ted a while to get chummy with Willow.

I made a decision. 'We want to take Pete home.'

Helen and her colleague were pleased, but especially Helen. It was clear that, in the short time she'd fostered

Pete, she'd developed a soft spot for him and whole-heartedly wanted him to go to a good home.

I wondered how the Battersea staff did their jobs, day in day out, and managed not to take home every animal that came into the Home.

Two days later, Dave and I returned to collect Pete. At the time, it was being considered whether Charlie, the dog that had found Pete, might appear in Paul O'Grady's TV show *For the Love of Dogs*, which was set at the Home, so we were filmed as we signed over the documents and as Pete was handed into our care. We would learn later if Charlie had made the cut.

When we got Pete home, Ted and he ignored each other. Considering the rough start Pete had had – we'd been told he'd been shoved into a bin and left to die – he seemed unfazed by all the change. He spent his waking hours sniffing and investigating everything. It was clear he was very nosy and didn't leave a cushion unturned, or a corner uninspected. When he was ready for a nap, he jammed himself into Ted's bed, regardless of what Ted thought, and snoozed.

Dave and I set about picking a name for him. We circled around 'Herbie' and various others but nothing seemed quite right. Then I said: 'Well, he was found in a bin and he's a bit scruffy-looking. What about Scrappie?'

Dave laughed but, no matter what other names we threw around, Scrappie was the one that stuck.

For the first three or four days, Ted was unsure of Scrappie and didn't make much effort with him. But one afternoon I was pottering about the house when I heard a crash, a bang and a soft, playful bark I recognized as Ted's. It was followed by a higher-pitched bark that came in threes.

I went into the kitchen to see Ted had Scrappie's bed in his jaws and was pulling Scrappie around the floor. For a minute Scrappie, being quite lazy and stubborn when he wanted to be, didn't show any reaction until, when Ted was least expecting it, he jumped out and tumbled past Ted, whose tail was wagging furiously with excitement. It was the first time I'd seen them playing together and I knew it was the start of something special.

Later, Ted was acting quite submissively to entice Scrappie into a tug-about, and when that didn't work, he took a more direct approach: he chased Scrappie round the coffee-table. That did work, and it was a joy to watch. It was especially sweet that Ted was having fun, and when Scrappie changed direction and chased Ted – beating him at his own game – it was clear we'd picked the right friend for him. After all, that was the whole point in our seeking out a puppy like Scrappie.

Scrappie had boundless energy and, once he had finished teasing Ted about whether or not he would play, Ted was committed to their games for hours. In time, the dynamics of our duo became more apparent. Ted wasn't as intelligent as Scrappie but he was super-friendly. While Scrappie would sit by the treats cupboard and bark to let me know he wanted one, Ted was more likely to be found in the neighbours' garden, eating the bird feed. Little Scrappie liked to have a good chase and a hunt. He was forever running around outside, barking at squirrels, then chasing them through the bushes and along the fence. The good thing about the dogs' differences was they didn't get in each other's way.

Before we knew it, Christmas was fast approaching. We didn't set up a tree or pull out stockings. Instead, we wrapped our presents, packed our car and, with Scrappie and Ted, set off for Dave's parents' home in Devon.

By now, I was seven months pregnant, and as we settled in over the weekend, my thoughts turned to all the changes coming our way. We had a gorgeous new home that Scrappie thoroughly enjoyed. Scrappie had become a great friend to Ted, and Dave and I knew we were expecting a little boy. The thought of the amazing year ahead was overwhelming, but before it had a chance to take hold, a little face appeared beside me. Scrappie had that mischievous look in his eye and was dying for a game. I tickled him and rolled his ball across the room. Back and forth he went, dragging it out from under the table and running back to me. He never tired of fetching it.

On Christmas morning I gave the boys their presents. I called Ted and placed a long, thick wrapped parcel in front of both dogs. Scrappie was straight on one end and Ted on the other. Seconds later, the festive wrapping was in shreds around us as Scrappie and Ted played tug of war with the colourful soft, knotted rope they now had in their jaws. It was good they had something to occupy them because Scrappie had been rummaging about under the Christmas tree ever since we'd arrived for the wrapped-up treats he could smell.

After Christmas dinner, which the boys slept through, we were all ready for a walk. It was a Christmas tradition for our family to head to the beach nearby with Ted and Willow. Scrappie was thrilled to see so many other dogs about and wanted to play with them all. But the minute his paws touched the cold water, he yelped and retreated at lightning speed. Unlike Ted, he hated it. I watched as Scrappie raced from dog to dog, convinced they all wanted to play, and when he barked, Ted barked too. Scrappie knew just how to lead Ted on, and after a while, I asked Dave to bring them in so we could go back to the house.

After the Christmas festivities, we returned home to Hampshire and, during the day, the boys played on our land. Every morning, they joined me to check on the sheep – twenty-five ewes and five lambs – and, to my delight, Scrappie followed Ted's example and didn't cause any trouble. They made me squirm when they ate sheep poo, but I was happy we'd been able to give Scrappie such a lovely, carefree lifestyle.

At the right time, I went into labour and soon returned home with our son, Oliver. When we got back from the hospital, Dave and I placed Oliver, still in his car seat, on the living-room rug. We didn't want to make a fuss but Ted and Scrappie needed to understand there was a new person in the house. They both rushed over, their tails wagging, and sniffed Oliver and his seat. When they realized he was a living, breathing thing, they were curious, but it wasn't long before they lost interest. We never left Oliver on his own with the dogs, and whenever they were near him, we were within grabbing distance. At night, we locked them into the kitchen so we knew they wouldn't venture upstairs to Oliver's room if he was crying.

With good reason: whenever Oliver cried, Ted was beside himself. He'd always been the type to rush to the TV if he heard a cry and now it was happening in his house.

He would rush to Oliver and then to me, begging me to follow him. When I reached Oliver, Ted got under my feet but I didn't tell him off. He was only worried and, in time, he calmed down. It was a matter of weeks before Ted figured out, as always long after Scrappie, that Oliver was not only here to stay, but his cries would be the recurring soundtrack in our home. He was soon ignoring them.

Now whenever Oliver is in my arms or on my lap, Ted will rest his head nearby and sniff Oliver's foot. Scrappie ignores him completely. He doesn't ignore Ted, though. I still find the pair of them playing in the kitchen and, when they think nobody is watching, snuggling up together in the living room. Scrappie is everything we hoped he would be for Ted, and now that Dave and I are busy with Oliver, he's a godsend.

I'm so glad we went back to Battersea and were matched up so perfectly. Seeing Helen that day and learning about her experience with Scrappie had been the deciding factor. I'm grateful to her and Battersea for helping our family grow in such a perfect way. In return, it is our pleasure to give Scrappie the life he deserves, after his shocking start, in a warm and loving home.

9. Start as You Mean to Go On . . .

With the crowds heaving closer around me, I reached to the ground and pulled a furry little form into my arms. With my Jack Russell Johnny Reggae safely tucked next to me, I began to sing, with the hundreds of other people around me.

> *This star drew nigh to the north-west;*
> *O'er Bethlehem it took its rest,*
> *And there it did both stop and stay,*
> *Right over the place where Jesus lay.*
> *Noel, Noel, Noel, Noel,*
> *Born is the King of Israel.*

It was my favourite Christmas carol and, despite the freezing temperatures, people had gathered for as far as the eye could see outside my local shopping centre to sing together at a charity fundraiser for a homeless centre.

Our breath shot out in puffs of swirly mist and our fingers ached from the cold, but when we met our neighbours' eyes we all smiled. It didn't matter that we were cold because it was Christmas and the air was zinging with excitement. A huge tree had been erected in the town centre, shimmering and sparkling with colourful lights and decorations.

Our singing continued and we all stared, mesmerized, at the open-top double-decker bus parked to one side: on the top deck the Archbishop of Canterbury led us in the carols and it was a wonderful, beautiful way to get ready for Christmas. The crowd around me boosted a local choir and, together, our voices soared into the night sky.

It was especially sweet for me because, in my arms, Johnny Reggae listened patiently and gazed around with eyes wide as dinner plates, soaking up the sights, sounds and smells. I could tell my boy was enjoying this as much as I was.

My husband Nick and I had adopted Johnny Reggae from Battersea Dogs & Cats Home a month earlier. He was seventeen and had had a hard life, but we were determined to give him every comfort and treat to see out his twilight years.

Nick was a divorce lawyer and I was a marketing consultant. We had toyed with the idea of getting a dog for a long time, and when I saw Johnny Reggae's profile on Battersea's website for six weeks in a row, I'd realized I wanted to be the one to give him a home. As soon as we'd picked him up he'd become the centre of our universe. We loved him to bits and so did everyone who knew us.

Now, the carol service had got me well and truly in the mood for Christmas, and a few days later, we packed our things and took Johnny Reggae to Liverpool to stay with Nick's parents over the festive period. My parents joined us there too and our newest family member took it all in his stride.

By Christmas Eve, everyone was saying Johnny Reggae was the best dog ever.

I told them: 'I know I'm biased but you are so right!' He was such a survivor and always made the right decision for himself. If a door was about to shut, he knew which side to be on when it did – if the kitchen was on one side, he'd choose that side because he loved his food and was led by the nose.

Johnny Reggae was spoilt rotten with treats and scraps from everyone at the dinner table. My parents adored him, my mum especially. Whenever she saw him, she said: 'Hello, my little pavement special.' She called him that because we weren't quite sure what mix he was. But it was very much a term of endearment.

On Christmas morning, my in-laws, parents, Nick and I gathered downstairs in the lounge by a beautiful gold-and-red-themed tree with dozens of presents crammed underneath. I reached in and grabbed a soft one I'd wrapped earlier for Johnny Reggae. I opened it and everyone laughed as I held out a miniature Father Christmas outfit, complete with a red cape and fur-trimmed hood. 'Sorry, Johnny,' I said, 'but I've got to see you in this.'

I pulled him into my lap and slowly dressed him in it. Once it was on, I turned him to face the waiting family and everyone was grinning. 'Don't you look great!' I told him.

But Johnny Reggae turned to me and let out a grumble. He refused to move and I could tell he hated the outfit. I took some pictures of him in it and could tell he was embarrassed, the poor soul.

That was the first and only time he growled at me. But it was harmless. Johnny Reggae had lost a lot of his teeth due to infection so he didn't have a single pair top and bottom that touched. It was his way of making clear his feelings on that outfit. I called him to me, and he co-operated while I took it off, standing still or lifting his leg when he needed to.

Once the outfit was off, Johnny Reggae didn't speak to me for a few minutes but he forgave me soon after. It just added to the fun.

As time went on, I learnt that he didn't like a fuss being made of him. He hated having his coat brushed and he definitely wasn't a lapdog. But without even trying, he made everyone he met fall in love with him. Even Nick, a no-nonsense Yorkshireman, was putty in Johnny Reggae's paws and they both knew it.

The moment Nick arrived home from work, Johnny Reggae raced to the larder where he knew his treats were kept. He had a problem with his spine that meant his tail didn't wag so instead his whole body moved from side to side. Whenever Nick treated him, he told me: 'It's ridiculous but I just can't resist that little face of his!'

Behind his soft moments, we came to understand Johnny Reggae's true nature. Despite the arthritis he suffered from, he was happy to go for two walks a day and trot along.

We took him for weekend breaks in the country or to the beach. He always wore the same defiant look on his face: *Yeah . . . not fussed.* Though he'd lived in London and we reckoned he probably hadn't seen any of these new things, he took everything in his stride.

When Johnny Reggae had an opinion, he told us loud and clear. If he didn't fancy a walk one day, he'd dig his heels in and refuse to budge from the front door. As time went on, he grew stiffer in his joints, hard of hearing, struggled to see and preferred snuffling around the garden. We put up screens to stop him hurting himself on the rosebushes so he'd find a spot in the sunshine and lie in it till he baked.

It brought me a lot of happiness to see him living the dream. He knew he'd lucked out when he came home to us and luxuriated in it. But I felt we were the ones who'd lucked out. Nick and I had spent many years building successful careers and finding the perfect home. We'd whizzed through life at such a fast pace that sometimes we didn't give ourselves time to enjoy the simple things we took for granted: a walk in the sunshine or relaxing at home.

It was only when Johnny Reggae had come to stay for good that we realized what we'd been missing out on. I cut back my hours and Nick worked from home whenever he could.

We were around in case Johnny Reggae needed us, and instead of pampering him, which he hated, we treated him to lovely food. To soothe his joints, we gave him oily fish.

Johnny Reggae had a ferocious appetite and downed food like a gannet. To help him burn off the weight he was so prone to gaining, I liked to walk him around the grounds of Canterbury Cathedral, which wasn't too far from our home. I loved the beautiful gardens and sometimes I'd sneak into the back of the cathedral with Johnny Reggae in my arms and we'd listen to choral evensong. When I held him close to me and savoured the beautiful singing – goose-bumps racing up and down my arms – Johnny Reggae closed his eyes and listened. It was loud enough for him to hear and feel. Afterwards, we'd take a seat on a bench in the cathedral's gorgeous walled garden and catch the last of the evening's sunshine. It was planted in such a way that all year round flowers would bloom.

Though we were trying to give Johnny Reggae the best in life, our lives were changing too. I was looking at things in a different light and appreciating things in a new way, things I probably wouldn't have noticed before, like the evensong or the pretty flowers in the garden.

In time, Johnny Reggae lost his sight completely. At home, we carried him up the garden stairs and set him down on the soft grass, then pulled plant pots in front of the steps to stop him trying to go up them. He learnt to get around.

His second Christmas was more subdued than the previous year. He was listless and didn't have any energy. I didn't tease him with *that* outfit and nothing we did or gave him roused his interest. On New Year's Eve, I abandoned dinner to take him to the vet.

'Stephanie, his liver isn't working properly,' the vet told me, 'but these pills should help.'

I took the prescription and Johnny Reggae home. Weeks passed, then months, and Johnny Reggae seemed to have lost his fight.

After a trip to Liverpool to see Nick's parents, we took him to the vet once more.

The vet examined him. 'He seems a bit dehydrated. Have you moved his water bowl?'

While we'd been with Nick's parents, Johnny Reggae hadn't remembered where his water bowl was and couldn't see it so now he was dehydrated. I felt guilty that I hadn't noticed and panicked that the mistake would cost Johnny Reggae dearly. We'd taken him on knowing we wouldn't have years and years with him, but now I didn't think I'd ever be ready to let him go.

Johnny Reggae was put on a drip and when I picked him up the next day, he was a new man. He was full of beans and had a new lease of life. It was such a relief. He pottered the days away in the garden, baking in the sunshine or snuffling around. He refused to go on any walks so I didn't force him. Nick and I agreed to give him whatever he wanted.

It was a September afternoon when Johnny Reggae sat down in the garden, then couldn't get up again. I nudged Nick, who was working outside on his laptop. 'Are you seeing this?'

He followed my gaze to Johnny Reggae. When he spoke, his voice was husky with holding back tears. 'If he's like this tomorrow, we'll make the decision,' he said.

I didn't say a word, just nodded.

'If he's not well, then it's not fair to him,' Nick added.

I don't know who he was trying to convince, me or him.

Next day, Nick was in court, and at three o'clock, I took Johnny Reggae into the garden, up the steps and set him down in the sunshine. Instantly, his back legs gave way and he sank down. He tried to push himself up again, then gave a sigh and lay down. That was when I knew.

I texted Nick: *The dog is bad and we need to take him to the vet. Will you be home by 7 p.m.?*

I paced in the garden while Johnny Reggae basked in the autumn warmth. I was desperate to hear from Nick. I held my phone in my hand and willed Nick to reply. *I can't do this alone.*

There was no reply from Nick so I went next door to speak to my neighbour, Sally. I was crying by the time I reached her door, and when Sally opened it, my words came out in a jumble. She had taken care of Johnny Reggae on days when Nick and I had been at work and she loved him very much. When she understood what I was trying to say, her eyes filled with tears. Arm in arm, we returned to my garden, sat on the bench and held Johnny Reggae. For once, he didn't try to get away, just leaned on me.

Sally and I cried together and then we booked an

appointment at the vet for later that evening. She promised to come with me if I didn't hear from Nick. I thanked her and told her I'd let her know when it was time to leave. Then I took Johnny Reggae into the kitchen and placed him on his bed. His eyes stayed on me as I pulled a packet of sausages out of the fridge and fried them all. This was going to be Johnny Reggae's last meal and I wanted it to be something he would love.

When it was ready, I sat on the kitchen floor and fed half the sausages to him. If he could have wagged his tail, I reckoned he would have – he enjoyed the sausages that much.

I packed up the rest and, just as we were about to leave the house, Nick texted: *I'm on my way, wait for me.*

When Nick arrived, we left the house together and headed to the surgery. They sedated Johnny Reggae and, as they did so, I treated him to another sausage. I stroked his head. 'You're such a lovely boy, Johnny Reggae, we really love you.'

Johnny Reggae was nineteen years old when he closed his eyes for the final time.

I began to cry and Nick pulled me into his arms. I couldn't believe it – just like that, the dog that had opened my eyes and made me appreciate the life I had with Nick was gone. We decided to have Johnny Reggae cremated, and the vet gave us the option of an individual cremation, which we took.

We went into the reception area and Nick asked the difference in price. It was expensive and I expected him to roll his eyes but, instead, he took a deep breath and said:

'That's fine.' He made the arrangements and we returned home.

Before I'd taken my shoes off, I cleared all Johnny Reggae's things away. I couldn't look at them and knew I would want to do it in the morning even less than I wanted to do it then.

I couldn't entertain the idea of coming downstairs to find his empty bed in the kitchen. *Better to get it over and done with.*

I packed away any dog food to give to friends who had pets and went to bed, totally heartsick.

I was in pieces for two days until his ashes were delivered in a little wooden container. It bore a simple brass plaque that read 'JOHNNY REGGAE'.

I held it for a while and, somehow, felt better. I placed it on the mantelpiece in the lounge and every time I walked past I blew him a kiss, then burst into tears. The sense of grief I had felt was disproportionate to what I had expected, and I didn't think people would understand. But, to my surprise, they did. I received so many cards from neighbours, friends and even parents of friends, sending me their heartfelt condolences. One wrote: *Johnny Reggae was such a beautiful dog. What a fantastic life you gave him in his twilight years. No one will ever forget him.*

It made me realize how many people had loved him and it meant a lot to me that everyone was being so kind. It didn't stop me feeling sad, though. At

Christmas I wrapped Nick's present and placed it under the tree.

On Christmas morning when he opened it to reveal a painting of Johnny Reggae, he grew very still. Then he looked up at me, eyes glistening with tears. 'He really was such a special chap.'

My face must have lit up because Nick smiled at me through his sadness. We shared our favourite memories of Johnny Reggae, and I said: 'He was a smashing dog, wasn't he?'

As the New Year hurtled towards us, I thought how lovely it would be to have another dog. A fresh start of sorts. It was nice to think we could do some good, too, by taking in another unwanted one. In January, Nick and I agreed to dip a toe in at Battersea's Brands Hatch branch and see what was available. That was when I saw a little dog that was ready for rehoming. She was a nine-year-old Jack Russell with a sweet little face and her name was Meggy. I called ahead and arranged to meet her.

When I arrived at the beautiful rural grounds of the Brands Hatch site, the rehomer told me Meggy's history and I knew instantly she wasn't right for Nick and me. She couldn't be left on her own. I met Meggy, as I'd come all the way there, but I had to tell the rehomer: 'It wouldn't be fair to another family if I took Meggy on. She's not right for us.'

The rehomer was understanding. 'Don't worry, we'll find her a home.'

Two days later when I checked the website, a red 'Rehomed' banner flashed across her profile.

About three weeks passed. Then, one day, my phone rang. When I answered, it was a rehomer from Brands Hatch. 'We've got a Jack Russell cross in and we think he might be a really good match for you.'

I was surprised to get the call, but so grateful and flattered that the staff had thought of me.

I learnt that Billy was a sweet little chap who'd had a rough time. The rehomer told me: 'He hasn't had much exposure to the real world, and the kennels aren't suiting him. We're hoping to rehome him quickly.'

My best friend Asha was coming to stay with me the following weekend while Nick was busy working so we decided to make the trip together to see Billy. Nick and I agreed in advance that if I liked Billy he'd go to meet him the following week and we'd take it from there.

On Sunday afternoon, Asha and I went to Brands Hatch and what we learnt about Billy was nothing we could have prepared for. It was beyond heartbreaking. Billy was eight and had been with the same family all of his life. He'd lived with a father and daughter, who had loved him very much, but the daughter had mental-health problems, which had made her unpredictable around the dog. In the last six months, she'd tried to hurt Billy three times.

I gasped when I heard that Billy, who loved the woman dearly, would be sitting on her lap enjoying a stroke when, all of a sudden, she'd turn against him.

The father had brought Billy to Brands Hatch even though he didn't want to give him up.

Now Billy was emotionally fragile, in desperate need of a loving new home. I really wanted to meet him so we were shown to the kennels. A lot of the dogs came forward to see us as we walked past, but when we arrived at Billy's kennel he didn't even look up. 'He's not liking this at all, the poor thing,' I said to Asha.

Asha, who is normally quite tough, was on the verge of crying.

'Can we please meet him properly?' I asked the rehomer.

We were shown to a meeting room and the rehomer fetched Billy for us. I was expecting a shy dog to come in, but the moment Billy entered the room, his tail was wagging and he looked so bright and excited. He jumped straight on to my lap, proud as you like, and settled there.

I thought: *We're taking this dog.*

It had been raining when we'd left the house so I'd worn my knee-high boots. Although it was very muddy outside, I took Billy for a walk in the fields, just the two of us. He didn't mind the mud, and neither did I, but I noticed he was very nervous. Every noise made him jump, and at times he looked like a rabbit in headlights. In fact, he was so nervy that he did everything at lightning speed. It was quite a change from Johnny Reggae, but Billy had found himself a home right in my heart.

He seemed so different from when I'd first seen him in the meeting room and I wondered if perhaps Billy

Above: Westie Jessie snoozing in the Cornwall sun. *Below:* Mongrel puppy Santa was brought into Battersea on Christmas Eve by a member of the public who found him wandering the streets of London.

Jack Russell cross Charlie stole the heart of Battersea's Liz and she gave him a permanent home.

It was on one of their walks that Liz came across the bin where Scrappie had been abandoned.

Long after Terry and Pat's children had flown the nest, Dancer the Akita cross puppy reminded the retired couple what it's like to have a child in the house once more.

Dancer, now called Sam, steals a nap on Terry and Pat's bed.

Dancer was only a foot tall as a puppy. Now he's three years old and doesn't know his own size!

Battersea's Elizabeth started fostering these tiny kittens when they were just two weeks old. Would she be able to give them up? *Above right:* The scales register a little under 200g.

A curious Olive emerges from the Christmas wrapping paper.

Olive and Ophelia are all grown up.

Rosie the Staffie was left fighting for her life after being thrown into a freezing lake.

Against all odds, Rosie survived the ordeal and, with Battersea's help, found a loving new home.

might not be as confident as he'd appeared to be. I returned to the main building and told the rehomer I wanted him. We agreed Nick would visit on Tuesday night while I was away with my horse, Lander, for a show.

When I returned home, Nick was working. Eventually he took a break and I made him a cup of tea. 'I really want this dog, Nick.'

'I'm sure I'll feel the same,' he said. 'I'll be at Brands Hatch on Tuesday night.'

That day, I was competing Lander in a dressage competition near Watford, Hertfordshire, and by the time I arrived home it was nearly seven o'clock. I opened the door, and when I got to the sofa I froze. Nick was sprawled on it and next to him was a brindled Jack Russell with a grey face.

'Billy!' I gasped, moving towards them in shock.

Nick was grinning from ear to ear and his eyes twinkled. 'I bet you didn't see that one coming, did you?'

I settled on the other side of him and swallowed the sudden lump in my throat. 'I really didn't.' It had been the biggest surprise but the best one I'd had in as long as I could remember.

Nick reached across Billy and squeezed my hand.

That evening, the three of us snuggled up on the sofa, all of us shattered. Nick and I were both coming down with flu. But Billy, whom we'd renamed Tiffin, because he was such a treat, stayed hunkered down between us. He was the opposite of Johnny Reggae. He loved to be stroked and cuddled, and wanted to be jammed up next to us, lying on his back.

I'd bought a large crate for him so I put his bed and a bowl of water in it, then him. Nick and I went to bed.

An hour passed and I woke to loud barking. Tiffin was three floors down but I could still hear him. 'Maybe he needs the loo,' I said, pulling on my dressing-gown. Nick was still fast asleep, and I envied his ability to sleep through anything.

I went downstairs to find Tiffin really distressed. I sat on the floor next to the crate and opened the door. He flew out and slammed into me, desperate for me to stroke him. If I stopped, he pawed at me and howled. I'd never had a dog before Johnny Reggae and he had been so relaxed about bedtime. I'd had no experience of this behaviour and was at a loss for what to do. I tried to comfort Tiffin but it was clear he simply didn't want me to leave him.

Then I had an idea. I turned on my laptop and Googled what to do. Every website I came across said I should shut Tiffin in the crate and walk away. I hesitated but I knew it was the right way to go about it.

I muttered, 'Start as you mean to go on,' then put Tiffin inside and shut the door.

As soon as my back was turned, he began to howl.

I shut the kitchen door, then went upstairs and shut the bedroom door. I got into bed, put earplugs into my ears and went to sleep.

Hours later I jolted awake and removed one of the earplugs. There it was. Tiffin was still going. But it was for the best he learnt straight away that night-time was crate-time.

Early next morning I went downstairs and Tiffin bounced with excitement. He jumped up and down on the spot but didn't try to climb up me. He was just so happy to see me.

Within two nights, he'd stopped howling. But during the day, if I was on the phone, he'd begin again. I ignored him and soon all the howling stopped.

It was as if he'd suddenly connected the dots. *Mummy and Daddy are here and they are not going anywhere.*

But that was the tip of the iceberg. We soon discovered that Tiffin's past had had a lasting effect on his behaviour in many ways. When I took him out for walks I noticed quickly that he hated being around other dogs. It was as if a red mist of rage gripped him whenever he saw another of his kind and he would go crazy. I had a theory that perhaps he'd not been around dogs or socialized much with them when he had been with his previous owners and that this had led to his fury when he saw one.

When a member of the Brands Hatch team called to see how we were getting along, I explained that Tiffin wasn't dealing well with other dogs. I talked to one of the behaviourists and he gave me some guidance. 'For the time being,' he said, 'try to walk in areas that are not heavily populated with dogs – woods, or parks that have large open spaces. That'll give Tiffin the chance to move away, if you do encounter another dog, and not be in a small space with it. You can walk along roads, too, but make sure you're aware of any dogs approaching and try to give them a wide berth.' It was common sense, really, I thought.

The trainer continued: 'I'd like you to work on making Tiffin focus on you. You need to get his attention and keep it. Reward him with a treat when he does what you want. Gradually, while you're practising this, build in distractions. Go to a place where you know there will be other dogs and reward him when he keeps his attention on you, rather than barking at them. If he does get vocal, work on his attention again, and keep trying. You'll get there in the end – Tiffin wants to please you. He just has to understand how to do it.'

There was work to do elsewhere too. 'He's a bright little dog,' the trainer observed. 'He needs plenty of mental stimulation when you're at home or in the garden, something to occupy his mind. He should enjoy search games – and many dogs love getting food out of kongs. You'll find one at your local pet shop.'

The trainer also told me to monitor Tiffin's behaviour carefully: he recommended that I kept a diary and noted down any changes in Tiffin's posture when he met dogs. That way I'd get an idea of whether or not he was making any progress.

Clearly it would take some time to figure out what Tiffin could and couldn't handle and, for now, we'd have to take the rough with the smooth. We noticed that Tiffin was nervous with women: if Nick and I were in a room, Tiffin would suddenly disappear behind Nick and cower. If I called him, he wouldn't come, but he quickly became besotted with Nick, to the extent that if we got home together and I opened the door, he would knock me down to get to Nick.

I felt sad for me and sad for Tiffin. I didn't want him to be scared of me, but he'd been traumatized by his past and that wasn't his fault. It explained why, that first night, though he was nervous with women, he'd still jumped into my arms. His need for comfort had outweighed his fear of me. I hoped that, in time, he'd come to learn that I would never hurt him and he was safe to love me as I loved him.

If Nick wasn't there, Tiffin was fine with me on my own, but every now and then, a noise or the jolt of a memory would trigger something and his ears would flatten, he'd look at me with wide eyes, then run away and hide.

I paid close attention to my own behaviour and questioned my actions a lot. Did I move too quickly? Did I catch him off guard? I wore my hair up, then down, trying to figure out his triggers but it was impossible to pinpoint. It took all I had not to cry when it happened – it made me so sad to think of what he'd suffered.

'What should I do?' I asked the dog trainer. 'Should I reassure him?'

He was firm: 'Dogs don't understand reassurance. You will only reinforce bad behaviour if you comfort him when he reacts negatively.'

'What's the alternative?' I queried.

'Ignore him until he comes to you, then make a big fuss of him.'

Inside I felt terrible for Tiffin and it went against my every instinct to ignore him when he was scared: he'd been abused by somebody he'd trusted and loved, and it was neither his fault nor hers. But it wasn't my fault either.

What a sad state of affairs.

Whenever Nick arrived home, Tiffin didn't want to know me any more. He wouldn't let me walk round his back end, and if I caught him unawares, he'd flinch and move away. I wondered if his tail had been pulled a lot. If I put his food in a bowl and set it in front of him, he'd watch me until I left the room before tucking in.

It was hard work and I felt deflated. When we went for a walk, every noise freaked him out. I told Nick: 'He's like a cat on a hot tin roof, he jumps that much.'

Whenever I got his lead he'd hop excitedly, but outside, when he realized we were leaving the house, he wouldn't budge.

But every now and then, Tiffin and I would have a lovely moment together, which made things worthwhile. In the summer I ventured further away from our home and found myself in the walled garden at the cathedral. Like Johnny Reggae before him, Tiffin sat on the bench with me and watched the world go by. It was such a peaceful place, not just for me but Tiffin too. He leant into me and let me stroke him from head to tail without flinching. It was an amazing feeling to have Tiffin start to trust me and relax around me. If he was spooked by a female friend or relative who came to our home, though, he would seek comfort from Nick, not me. I learnt to accept that.

In time, Nick and I took Tiffin to dog-training classes every Sunday and, at first, we couldn't join in, just walked around the periphery so Tiffin could get used to seeing other dogs.

Slowly, things started making sense to him. He no longer went crazy when he saw another dog and we were able to complete two forty-five-minute walks with him each day. If somebody had a dog that set Tiffin off, I'd shout: 'Sorry, he's a work-in-progress.' Everybody understood. I was seeing the same faces every day and found myself making new friends while I was out and about with Tiffin. His horizons were expanding and so were mine. It felt nice to be on this journey together. In the mornings, I took to running with Tiffin and he seemed calmer like that. When he saw other dogs, we were already down the road when he remembered to bark. Every morning I'd pull on my running shoes and Nick laughed. 'Rather you than me,' he said. But, actually, I was glad it was me: Tiffin was already besotted with his dad. I had to work for his love.

It was then that the real Tiffin began to show. He's very needy of people and of love, but he's quite capable of being left on his own for a couple of hours. But if you're there, he wants you constantly. Tiffin nudges you politely, then stares at you endlessly till you give him some love.

With his eyes opened to the world and experiencing more things in the short months he'd been with us than he probably had in is whole lifetime, he started to man up. He was still fragile, but he grew bolder, more confident. He bounded around the house and garden like he owned the place.

When we went to my parents' home, he followed my dad everywhere he went. When I called him back, Tiffin ignored me. I called him again and he ignored me a second time. I said firmly: 'Bad dog.' That stopped him in his tracks. When he moved again, it was towards me. The minute I said, 'Good boy,' he rushed off after Dad again.

I waited till he was out of earshot, then laughed. The little sausage was testing me and, in an odd way, that was a good thing. It showed he was starting to feel confident around me, secure enough to show me how he felt about things. As long as he was still following instructions, I reckoned that was fine. We didn't have to agree on everything.

Gradually he became more and more comfortable with me. It was as if he was starting to see that nothing bad would happen to him around me, and I was honoured that he was giving me that trust.

Nick and I love having Tiffin around. Tiffin is still very much a work-in-progress. If he gets frightened, he forgets how to behave, but he has lots of good qualities too. I'm teaching him to sit, come and wait. He is proving himself to be a sweet and gentle boy, and every morning when the alarm goes off, I can't wait to go downstairs and see him. When he's at doggy daycare, I miss him. He's really settled now. He knows that this is his home and that nobody is going to hurt him. Just like Johnny Reggae before him, everybody loves Tiffin.

Having Tiffin in our lives has been a learning curve: it's opened our eyes to the fact that not all dogs from Battersea are happy and self-assured, like Johnny Reggae was, in the beginning. Dogs like Tiffin need owners like us who are willing to take on the challenge and, with the support of Battersea, work out what the dog needs to give it a happier, secure and settled life.

The problems Nick and I encounter now pale into insignificance when Tiffin is with us, and I don't regret for a second taking on a dog with the difficulties he's had. He needed another chance. It's been our honour to help him find himself and enjoy life. We'd do it all again in a heartbeat.

10. A Life-changing Decision

It was early on an August morning when I got a call from my mum: 'Elizabeth, the cat's not well. I think it's time.'

I was so sad to hear that. In recent weeks, our cat Phoebe had gone from being well to extremely unwell. Even though she was eighteen and had come to the end of her natural life, her rapid deterioration had come as a shock to my parents, and an even bigger shock to me.

Phoebe had been our cat since 1998 when we'd gone to pick her from all the other cats at Battersea Dogs & Cats Home in Old Windsor. She'd been the quiet, pretty one whose eyes had followed our every movement until she'd stood up and tentatively rubbed her face against our outstretched hands. Now, fifteen years later, it was my task to take her to the vet and say goodbye. Though it was a summer's day, the heavens opened and rain fell as I left the clinic knowing I'd never see Phoebe again. Mum, Dad and I felt crushed and empty.

As long as I could remember, we'd had cats in our home. The first I'd known was a rescue tabby tom called Tigger, who'd come to stay when I was two years old and was with us for seventeen years. During Tigger's time, my grandmother's cat, Jasper, also came to live with us, then Oliver, another rescue – a ginger – and next our darling Phoebe. With the last of our family cats gone, I threw myself into my job – it was the only way I knew how to cope.

The irony wasn't lost on me that, after a lifetime of loving cats, I'd been lucky enough to get a job at Battersea Dogs & Cats Home. Previously, I'd worked in museums and galleries, promoting events and exhibitions, and now I was part of the marketing team at Battersea. There, the walls were lined with Battersea posters, and the mugs in the kitchen bore pictures of the cats and dogs from our various campaigns. The entire staff is animal crazy and it was a comfort to go to work every day.

My job kept me busy managing campaigns and overseeing the social media and website, so I got to meet and promote a lot of the animals waiting for new homes in the kennels or cattery. The job was busy and intensely satisfying but every now and then, I'd wander from our offices to the cattery. There I'd gaze at all the cats waiting for new homes and wish that I had the space to take one for myself.

I desperately wanted another cat but I was living in a rented flat with no outdoor space. Working full time, it didn't make any sense for me to have one, but I couldn't help how I felt.

That was when I got to know about Battersea's fostering scheme. It included hand-rearing kittens, if necessary, and when I heard about it, I put my name forward as a staff volunteer. On the call list, we were all waiting and ready to take on any new cats that needed a temporary home or extra care.

It was a blistering bank holiday Monday when my phone rang. I answered and listened as one of the cattery staff told me of a situation that had come up. 'We've had a litter of eight kittens come in. Their mother abandoned them and the owner doesn't know what to do. They all need hand-rearing. Can you help?' The kittens were only two weeks old and needed feeding every two hours, day and night.

I said: 'Of course. I'll be there as quick as I can.'

When I arrived, security buzzed me in and I went to the second floor of the cattery where mums and kittens are usually housed. I was shown to a pod with eight tiny kittens in it. I was given two black ones and a black-and-white one to take home, along with kitten formula and a box of other things I'd need. One of the black ones was so weak and tiny she couldn't hold her head up.

The foster co-ordinator said: 'It's very possible that that little one won't make it through the night. She's the smallest of them all.'

'I'll do my best.'

When I arrived home, it was already time for the kittens' next feed. I made up the formula and, using a plastic syringe, I fed them. The littlest one barely took any milk but I persevered throughout the night.

Next day, the kittens came to work with me and I handed them over to the veterinary nurses, who would take over looking after them in the clinic for the day. Other staff, who also had kittens from the litter, brought them in each day and they were kept as a group, with little tags on them to tell them all apart.

At lunchtime, I checked in on them, and after work, I took them home. The tiny one was managing to feed a little and was just about getting by.

A few days later, I was advised to hand over one of my three to a colleague who had just one. It's best to keep young kittens in pairs for company, so I gave up one of the bigger two. We weren't meant to get attached to our foster kittens but it was hard not to, and I already felt an affinity with the tiny one. I'd also been advised not to give the kittens any names, but I reckoned a nickname was OK . . .

I called the little black one Special, because she really was. Even though she was so tiny, she wasn't giving up and had so much fight in her. The other one, black-and-white, the biggest of the litter, became known as Beast for her size and matching appetite.

At bedtime, I set two-hourly alarms and woke to feed Special and Beast in the dead of night, just like you would a baby, except these babies needed only three millilitres of kitten milk. I encouraged them to go to the toilet by rubbing wet cotton wool on their bottoms and bathing them in warm water.

Steadily, the kittens grew stronger and their feeds went to every three hours, then every four, and they were drinking more and more milk.

After a month, I was able to start Special and Beast on solid food. To make the move easier for them,

I added a little kitten milk to the food to make the smell more familiar to them and encourage them to eat it. Like a proud new mum, I took them with me wherever I went in their carrier and they met lots of new people.

Although they were both growing stronger, worry was gnawing away at me.

When the time came, how would I bring myself to give them back? Hand-rearing them, I was falling in love with them and, naturally, they were very attached to me too. By now I had been allowed to give them proper names to help identify them in preparation for rehoming. As Battersea litters are each allocated a letter from the alphabet and these were the 'O Kittens', I had renamed Beast, 'Olive', and Special, 'Ophelia'.

I began asking my friends if they would be interested in taking on the kittens so at least I might be able to see them from time to time after they were rehomed. They were sympathetic but no one could help.

I began to feel desperate. *What was I going to do?*

I took the kittens to my parents' home in Shropshire one weekend, and as Mum held them, I said: 'They're so lovely, don't you want to keep them?'

Mum shook her head. 'With your sister's baby here now, I want to be able to visit her whenever I need to without worrying about what to do with any cats I might have. It's not the right time for us.'

I tried everything to talk her round but even tears didn't help. Mum wouldn't budge and I knew it was a lost cause.

Meanwhile, the kittens were getting bigger and running around my flat. Already, they were close to outgrowing it – they were literally climbing the walls. At eight weeks old they would have their injections and be ready to go out . . . and be rehomed.

It was a ticking time bomb hanging over my head.

One night, after a long day at work, I came home with them and, after feeding them, sat with them sprawled around me on the sofa. I looked around the tiny flat I called home and decided it was time to make some serious changes. I'd been saving up to buy a house for a long time and now I had two perfect reasons to get myself into gear. Next day, I made arrangements to speak to a mortgage adviser and made an appointment at the bank. After much discussion they agreed to give me a mortgage. Days later I went to the cattery and asked if it was possible to place the kittens on hold for me: I was actively looking for a house or a flat with a garden so that I could keep them. In the meantime I'd continue to foster them. They agreed.

I knew I wouldn't find a property overnight, but I wasn't going to waste any time. I signed up to every estate agent I could find, and every Saturday I viewed seven or eight properties in the hope of finding the perfect place.

In every single one, I thought: *Where would the cat beds go? What about the cat flap? Is it on a main road? Is the garden suitable?*

Nothing was quite right until I came across a little

house in Plumstead, Greenwich. As I flicked through the pictures of a 1930s house, I felt a tingle spread up my fingers and into my arms – this was the one.

I called the agent. 'I'd like to see this house, please.'

'I'm sorry, but an offer has already been accepted on it. It's no longer available.'

I was gutted. Maybe it wasn't meant to be. Maybe I wasn't going to find a house or make these two gorgeous kittens my own. Maybe it was all just a pipe-dream that was way out of my reach. I was at a loss for what to do.

A week later, at work, my mobile rang. It was the estate agent in Plumstead. He said: 'The offer has fallen through on that house and I wanted to give you first refusal to view it.'

I jumped at the chance and booked in for a viewing that weekend.

As soon as I walked in, I smiled. The house was homely and warm, just like my nan and granddad's. It was very old-fashioned, with nooks and crannies filled with trinkets and treasures. It needed a lot of work, but I could see its potential and charm. Outside, it had a big garden with a kitchen door that led straight into it – perfect for a cat flap. In fact, the whole house was absolutely perfect for the kittens and me.

I didn't need to think about it. There and then, I put in an offer, and hours later the owners called to tell me it had been accepted. I was absolutely elated.

'Thank you so much,' I said.

I returned home to the kittens and scooped them

into my arms. 'I've found our new home! You're not going to believe what we've got. You're so lucky, you two!'

Now all I had to do was convince the rehoming team I was right for the kittens.

On Monday morning, I went to straight the cattery and made my case for keeping them both. I told the rehomer: 'I've bought a house with a garden so that hopefully I can keep Olive and Ophelia.' I was so tantalizingly close to my dream that my eyes filled with tears and my voice cracked as I said: 'Can I please keep them?'

She could see I was getting upset so she put her hand on my shoulder. 'I'll have a chat with the team and we'll get back to you as quickly as we can.'

I returned to my office and tried to get on with my work but it was so distracting and nerve-racking waiting for the cattery's answer. Every time my phone rang I jumped. Hours later, the call I was waiting for finally came: 'There's no question. Of course you can keep the kittens.'

I was so happy I burst into tears at my desk.

Later, I flipped through my calendar to mark down all the important dates and realized it was exactly a year to the day that I'd started working at Battersea, and today I had become the proud new owner of two gorgeous Battersea kittens: Olive and Ophelia.

It was some time before I was able to move into my new home. Three months later, as Christmas approached, I began to pack my things. Olive and Ophelia – I call her Ophie for short – were little terrors, constantly in and out of the boxes in the flat, covering them with kitten bite marks. Every roll of wrapping paper and Christmas card had kitten teeth holes in it but I loved their mischief.

The knowledge that they were staying with me permanently made me so happy that they could have chewed through everything I owned and I wouldn't have minded.

And, by now, their personalities were really shining through.

Olive was quite needy: the moment she saw me she would climb up my trouser legs to get as close to my face as possible. She liked to wrap herself round my neck like a scarf, rubbing my face, or would sit on my shoulder as I walked around, like a little parrot cat. Ophelia was much more independent and would happily disappear on her own, either amusing herself with a toy or climbing into places she shouldn't.

In many ways they were like chalk and cheese but, unlike every other cat I'd known, they had both developed a love of water – they would jump under the shower with me or sit in the sink asking for the taps to be turned on. This was probably as a result of the warm baths I'd given them when I'd hand-reared them and was just one of their quirky little tricks.

I'd also managed to teach them both to give high fives for treats and took much joy in showcasing their talents to anyone who visited.

After I'd finished packing, I placed the kittens in their carrier and drove to my parents' home for

Christmas. My sister, Emily, her husband, James, and their baby, Miles, came too and we had a lovely time at Mum and Dad's. Their house is in the Shropshire countryside and at that time of year it's gorgeous. The fields have frosted tips and the rolling hills are stunning in the low winter sunshine.

Inside, the log fire was blazing, the Christmas tree was twinkling and we were enjoying a very special Christmas together: this year we had three new babies in the family – Miles, Olive and Ophelia.

On Christmas Day, we woke early to get dinner started, then had breakfast and sat down to open our presents. Emily and I passed out the presents from under the tree until each of us had a pile of gifts in front of us – even the kittens had their own little stack. We took turns opening them one at a time and the kittens raced around us, jumping in and out of boxes.

Miles, who was six months old, giggled hysterically whenever he heard wrapping paper tearing, and the kittens pounced on every scrap. They opened their gifts too, and since we'd soon be moving into our new home they received brand new matching bowls and beds, as well as treats, and toys to play with once we'd arrived.

It was a magical time for our family, filled with the joys of new life and new beginnings, and I knew in my heart that the year ahead was going to be a very special one. I'd taken on a mammoth task with the new house, as every inch of it needed redecorating, but it all felt very grown-up and satisfying.

After we'd opened our gifts, we had Christmas

dinner – the kittens couldn't believe their luck when they were treated to turkey titbits. At home they only had dry cat food and treats – I'm vegetarian – so they'd never tasted meat before. If the look on their faces was anything to go by, they were in kitty heaven.

Later, we settled in front of the telly to watch *Paul O'Grady: For the Love of Dogs at Christmas.* Along with other people from work, I was remotely looking after Battersea's social media. While I tapped away on the laptop, answering viewers' questions about the animals on the show, Olive was wrapped around my neck and Ophelia was lying beside me. With Battersea's supporters online, I posted behind-the-scenes facts and extra pictures for them to enjoy. It was heart-warming to be able to share the extra information with the viewers – they cared so much about what became of the animals at Battersea. I was really chuffed to have two of my very own right there with me.

On Boxing Day, I said my goodbyes and, with the kittens in their carrier, set out on the long journey home. This time, we weren't going to a small flat, but to our new house in south-east London. The previous owners had kindly left me quite a bit of furniture, so when we went inside, I set the carrier on the sofa in the living room and opened its door.

Olive bounded out and began jumping around in excitement and exploring her new surroundings. Ophie followed more slowly and carefully sniffed around.

As I set about unpacking, the kittens were leaping in and out of the boxes again, leaving fresh toothmarks on everything. There were many times I stopped what I was doing, looked at them and our new home and choked back tears. They had made me take responsibility and move forward with my life. I was no longer dreaming of owning my own home and having cats: I had done it.

Soon the kittens were spayed, and a month later, they were ready to go outside. Before I let them out, though, I went into the Battersea shop at work and bought a cat flap. I was no dab hand at DIY but I was determined to fit it myself. I banged and I sawed and I screwed it into place in the kitchen door. Then I stood up and grinned. 'That looks straight, doesn't it?' The kittens rubbed themselves around my legs. 'I'll take that as a yes, shall I?'

I took a picture of the cat flap and texted it to Mum. She texted back: *Well done, girls!*

Next, I popped a collar each on Olive and Ophelia – their first – then a harness. One at a time, we set off for a stroll around the garden. It wasn't the usual way to let your cats out but I was so worried about them disappearing that I couldn't bring myself to let them out on their own yet in case they went too far and got lost.

They were fascinated by the outside, and next time, I let them go free. The hours ticked by and I waited nervously. I was like a worried mum the first time her teenager goes out for a night on the tiles. Except my babies were kittens and they weren't painting the town red, they were snooping around our neighbours' gardens, literally just metres away.

At dinnertime I stepped into the garden, hoping

they'd be waiting for me, but there was no sign of them. I waited for a few minutes, then shouted: 'Olive! Ophie!'

When I heard the worry in my voice, I thought: *Oh, God. I've become one of those really annoying cat people!*

With a rustle to the left of me, one gorgeous little face appeared, then another. The kittens raced towards me and, after a quick stroke, dashed inside for food.

I came to learn quite quickly that Ophelia was very good at disappearing on her own. They were friendly too, because they'd been handled by me and many others in the first eight weeks of their lives. That is by far the best period to socialize cats, and my two were no exception. They were so friendly to any visitors and would happily stop by neighbours, pottering in their gardens, for a cuddle. I felt like a proud parent.

Whenever I got home from work, I whistled as I made my way down the road to the house, and Olive and Ophelia would come rushing out to escort me home.

If people asked what it was like having the kittens, I told them categorically: 'I've never been happier.'

And it was true.

This time last year, if someone had said I'd be in my own house with two cats, I wouldn't have believed them. But Olive and Ophelia came along and changed my life.

Some time later, I looked at their files at work to find out exactly when the kittens had been born and discovered something amazing. The kittens' birthday was 5 August 2013 – the very day we lost Phoebe. It made me go all funny when I read that. It was as if those kittens were meant to be mine.

11. Another Heartbeat in the House

It was early Sunday morning but in our house everyone was already awake. As we prepared to go to the stables to see our horses, four paws pounded impatiently by the front door. Our Boxer, Lenny, couldn't wait to get out. As soon as the door was opened, he was off like a shot.

As I watched my wife, Amanda, my daughter, Megan, and Lenny disappear down the road, near our home in Reading, Berkshire, a funny feeling swept over me.

To look at our handsome Lenny, you'd never guess that a dark cloud hung over him. Lenny was living with aspergillosis, a tissue-destroying fungal infection. It was a life-limiting disease, which caused him to have visible symptoms, such as a runny or bleeding nose, most days. He was heavily medicated to keep it, and his pain, under control but we all knew that, one day, it would claim him.

I pushed away the thought that, sooner rather than later, he'd be gone. That Sunday, and many more weekends to come, we continued our usual routine with Lenny because we were determined to give him the best quality of life with plenty of love, care and attention.

Time passed, and when Lenny was six, he started suffering seizures, a late-stage symptom of the disease.

We took him to the Cambridge Animal Hospital, which had provided him with excellent care throughout his life. Amanda and I said our tearful goodbyes to our faithful, gentle giant of a dog.

When we returned home, there was a deafening silence. Worse, our home was filled with all of Lenny's things, many of which had barely been used – some were still brand new. One Saturday morning, not long after we had lost him, I boxed up all of his belongings and we drove to nearby Battersea Dogs & Cats Home in Old Windsor.

We wanted to donate Lenny's belongings to somewhere we knew would make good use of them.

While we were there, I told Amanda: 'It wouldn't hurt to have a look around the kennels.'

She raised an eyebrow. We both knew we were not emotionally ready to take on another dog and maybe we never would be. Still, we strolled around the kennels and it was then I spotted this big old dog. She was a light-brindle Bull Mastiff and her name was Pepper. I approached her kennel and she rose on her back legs, looked me in the eyes and, her tail wagging, gave me a cuddle through the bars.

Pepper was beautiful. I stood closer to her than I should have done and talked to her for a while as her intelligent eyes watched me with curiosity. There and then, I could have taken her home. Amanda wasn't sure so, with a heavy heart, I walked away from Pepper.

Really, I knew Amanda was right to be wary of moving too quickly. For the last two years, we'd paid up to eight hundred pounds a month for Lenny's care, so not only were our hearts broken, but our bank account was depleted. We needed some time to regroup.

But there was a problem.

Our trip to Battersea had set us thinking about rehoming a dog. We didn't know what to do for the best so we talked about it late into the night. We wanted to help another animal, as we had Lenny, to take in a needy dog and give him or her our love and attention. That might prove to be Lenny's legacy. I told Amanda: 'We could give another dog a great life, like the one we gave Lenny.'

She agreed.

We both knew that even though Lenny had been ill for a number of years, we'd done everything in our power to give him the best quality of life. Deep down, we both wanted to do it again. Amanda and I registered our details with Battersea, in case a suitable dog came up in the future.

For us, it was the right way forward. We'd bought Lenny from a breeder, and when he became ill, he was MRI-scanned and X-rayed. We had learnt that the deformities in the structure of his skull were due to years of intensive breeding. Neither of us had associated that kind of deformity with a handsome dog like Lenny. In fact, Lenny's mother and father had both been pedigree show-winning dogs, but selective breeding can accentuate both desirable and undesirable traits. The breeding process left us with several unanswered moral questions.

Now, as I completed our Battersea application, I felt sure that a mixed-breed rescue dog would suit us, and that Battersea was the best place to begin our search.

Later we were interviewed, vetted and approved and took our time over deciding exactly when to bring a new dog home.

On 23 December, Amanda kissed me goodbye and went off for her late shift as a police officer at two p.m. Hours passed, and at ten, I received an email from her – she was having a quiet moment at work: *Our house isn't the same without that extra heartbeat. What do you think about the third one from the left?*

I scrolled down and there on the screen was an image that made me smile. It was a professional photograph of eight beautiful champagne-coloured puppies. The litter had been abandoned and now Battersea was rehoming them, according to a story in the *Daily Mail*.

I replied to Amanda: *He looks lovely. I'm ready if you are.*

The puppies were adorable, but they'd featured in a national newspaper. I didn't hold out much hope that they would still be available. Nevertheless, I logged into the Battersea website and registered my interest, using the profile we'd created months earlier.

Amanda also made an email enquiry. We kept our fingers crossed that one of us would get lucky.

The next day, on Christmas Eve, Amanda set off for work at eight a.m. Two hours later, she called me. 'You're not going to believe this, Jeff, but I've just had a call from Battersea. They said we can come in and meet the puppy we wanted from the photo. And if the meeting goes well, we can bring him home today!'

Apparently, there had been an outbreak of kennel cough at Battersea and they wanted the puppies rehomed without delay. The one we'd asked about was called Prancer, after one of Father Christmas's reindeer.

When we'd started our search, we'd never expected to have a new puppy in time for Christmas, but we were not about to say no!

Amanda booked the rest of the day off work and, though I was in the middle of painting our new bathroom in time for Christmas visitors – a bit of a departure from my day job as a surveyor – I downed tools and jumped into the car with Megan. We made a quick stop in Maidenhead to pick Amanda up, then drove into London. As we got nearer, the traffic on the motorway ground to a halt. It was getting later and later, and our deadline was fast approaching.

All the way there we hoped Battersea would wait for us. We wanted desperately to get there in time and it felt as though things were falling apart. I encouraged Amanda to call the Home and let them know we were on our way but stuck among thousands of other motorists travelling to their families for Christmas. Battersea had told us that they would be closing their doors at four o'clock.

I reached across the gear stick and took Amanda's hand in mine. 'Please don't upset yourself,' I said, 'I'm going to get us there. This puppy is coming home with us today.'

Amanda nodded, but she didn't say a word, although I could see she was getting more and more stressed. In the back, Megan was quiet, believing we had lost our chance.

At seven minutes past four, we pulled up outside the Home. Amanda and Megan were close to tears. 'We're too late,' Amanda said, as we raced towards the security booth. To our joy, we were ushered through.

We arrived at the desk and told the receptionist our names. She looked us up on the system and, with a smile, said: 'We're all ready for you.'

A rehomer took us to a side room and we sat down. Minutes later, she had returned with Prancer. She came towards us and placed him gently on Amanda's lap.

He looked like the Andrex puppy in the TV adverts.

The rehomer said: 'Spend some time with him and see how you bond.' She sat with us and chatted as Prancer got to know us a bit. He was calm and well behaved, and treated us to sloppy kisses. The bonding we would have hoped to come gradually was happening before our eyes.

We all cuddled him and Megan, who was on Christmas holidays from school where she was studying for her AS levels, had already fallen for him. He was so adorable, who wouldn't?

When it became clear that we wanted to take Prancer home with us, we were joined by one of Battersea's vets. 'I think Prancer and the rest of his litter are a mix of Akita, Foxhound and Staffordshire Bull Terrier,' he said. 'We don't know for sure, but that's what we think.'

He continued: 'See how you go with him, but if he is an Akita, you might have to deal with some stubbornness and a very strong will, so be prepared for that.'

Nothing could have changed our minds about Prancer now, and Amanda spoke up: 'We'd love to have him.'

We filled in the necessary forms and popped into the Battersea gift shop while the vet micro-chipped Prancer. There, we bought our puppy some toys and also picked up some of the Battersea children's story books for our two young nieces, who loved dogs just as we did.

Though the Home was closed, the staff were still busy. Everywhere you looked, staff and volunteers were moving around the site. It was only now that I noticed the jingly Christmas music playing softly in the background and the brightly coloured tinsel in the reception area. I realized that we were about to embark on a very special Christmas.

As we were preparing to leave with Prancer, the rehomer told us: 'This little dog will need a quiet environment without too much excitement or too many people.'

Amanda, Megan and I knew that would be difficult to achieve, given that it was Christmas and our family were coming to stay, but we promised to do our best. It was an unusual situation for Battersea – they didn't normally rehome animals so close to Christmas for exactly those reasons – but this year the kennel-cough virus could have proved fatal for any of the puppies if they had caught it.

On the way home, while I drove and Megan held Prancer, Amanda was making calls. She told all our family and friends about our new arrival, and warned those coming for dinner the next day that it might be a bit later than usual. We'd dropped everything to rush to Battersea, leaving paint pots and brushes in the bathroom, and a mountain of unpeeled spuds and vegetables in the kitchen. The Christmas tree wasn't even up!

When we arrived home, we made up a bed for Prancer in a quiet, open area under the stairs and set to work. Immediately, we were one pair of hands down. Amanda couldn't keep away from Prancer so I left her to it.

To our amazement, he was very well behaved from the start. He wasn't hyperactive, happily accepting cuddles and kisses or napping in his bed. Occasionally, he had a sniff around or pawed a bauble but quickly settled back in his bed. He'd had an exciting and tiring day.

Slowly but surely, the house took shape. While Megan finished putting the last baubles on the tree, I put up the Christmas lights and lit the fire.

Long after Prancer was asleep and Megan had gone to bed, Amanda and I finished peeling the potatoes and preparing the vegetables. It was two a.m., and we were exhausted so we went to bed. Just a few hours later, we were up again. We had eight coming for dinner, including my son Charlie, who lived and worked at Basingstoke Hospital, and my elder daughter Kayleigh, who arrived from Oxford in time for breakfast. They were both excited to meet Prancer, fussing and cuddling him. No matter how much we wanted to follow Battersea's advice to give him a quiet environment, it simply wasn't possible on Christmas Day.

Christmas is a big deal in our family, and as the day went on, Prancer coped well. He wasn't nervous or edgy and loved all the attention he was getting. He was starting to find his way around the house and was sniffing all the furniture. Prancer didn't run up to people: instead he waited till they were near him before he rolled over to have his belly rubbed.

Before dinner, we opened our presents, and because Prancer had been such a late addition to our family, Amanda, Megan and I had only the toys we'd bought for him from the Battersea shop.

But someone had done much better than that. Kayleigh, who was animal mad, pulled out a stocking filled with puppy treats, chews and toys and set it in front of him.

'I picked it up yesterday for him when Amanda called from work. I knew from the tone of her voice she was bringing him home for sure.'

It was the perfect gift but, after a cursory sniff, Prancer wasn't interested. He much preferred walking around, getting kisses and strokes from our guests.

As for the rest of us, the presents didn't matter because we had that gorgeous puppy! Everything had happened in such a blur – we had to keep pinching ourselves to be sure he was really ours.

With the fire blazing in the grate, Prancer took the same spot in front of it that Lenny always had and went to sleep while we sat down to a lovely meal. Despite all the drama, it was only an hour later than usual.

Afterwards, we started to think about what we should name our puppy, but nothing seemed to fit his character. We wanted somehow to link him to Lenny – we had named him after Lenny, the gentle giant in the Steinbeck novel *Of Mice and Men*. We considered George, Lenny's friend in the book, but George's stern character didn't suit our bouncy puppy.

Later in the evening, we watched an old film, as we always do. This year *It's A Wonderful Life* was showing. It's the story of a small-town bank manager who has to fight off the big-city lenders who are trying to buy his bank and make his customers' lives a misery. We'd seen it a hundred times, but everyone gathered in the lounge, taking a spot on the sofa or on the floor.

As the movie got under way, I noticed that George Bailey, the main character, was kind and benevolent. It gave me an idea. 'What about if instead of George we call the puppy Bailey? It still kind of links back to Lenny and George, and George Bailey is so kind.'

There was a moment's quiet as we all thought about it. Then there was a round of nods. With that, I scooped our puppy into my arms and looked at him. He looked like a Bailey so it was settled.

After the film, we played board games and, come midnight, everyone was suitably exhausted. We took ourselves off to bed, and Bailey slept straight through the night.

In the morning, we found him awake and in bed,

with the laziest expression on his face. This became a pattern. Every morning Amanda or I had to drag Bailey outside. He was the least demanding dog I'd ever known! At night, though, he began to keep a keen eye on the door and an ear to the ground for any movement outside. The moment he heard something, he let out a bark: *Something's going on.*

We told him: 'Thanks for your input, Bailey, but don't worry about that.'

Reassured, he went back to sleep.

As Bailey grew, his Akita traits started to show. He was protective and independent. He wasn't needy and didn't come to us all the time for cuddles. Instead, he patrolled the house day and night, checking on things. There were moments, of course, when he would roll over and wait for you to tickle his stomach. That was when he was at his most relaxed and he'd let out a funny sing-song type of soft howl – his Staffie side coming out. It was endearing and the best way to tell that Bailey was happy.

Outside the house, we learnt something else. When it came to other dogs, Bailey wasn't very sociable. As a puppy he'd been fearless and bounded up to dogs double his size to play. Now that he was nearing 30 kilos, it came off somewhat differently. He was very stubborn, just as the Battersea vet had predicted, and if the dog he approached didn't want to play, Bailey wouldn't leave them alone. We learnt it was best to move him on before things became heated.

As there hadn't been time for him to be neutered at

Battersea, because of the threat of kennel cough, we had him done when he was around a year old. After that, he was a bit less strong-willed and we found that other dogs didn't react to him in the same way as before. They weren't so argumentative around him and things calmed down.

It was then that Bailey's comical side began to shine. If he had picked an awkward spot to have a sleep, you couldn't move him. He was really talkative too. He grumbled and chatted and howled when he wanted something, usually his ball. He'd roll it around until it spun under the sofa or a cabinet and then he'd lie on the floor and grumble till one of us got down on our hands and knees to pull it out. He thought it was a terrific game, and once he was on a roll, he drove us mad with that ball.

Bailey was so communicative that he'd look at you when you talked to him, and howl back. Once, after watching a bunch of YouTube videos of dogs making sounds like human words, we thought we'd give it a try with Bailey. I sat on the sofa and he rested his front paws on my knees as I talked to him. 'Bailey,' I said, 'where does your aunty live?'

He began to howl.

I asked him again and then Bailey made a sound that had us all in stitches. So I asked him once more. He repeated it.

Bailey was saying: 'Bedford.'

We had great fun with that.

Bailey was not good around horses. Unlike Lenny, he

couldn't grasp that they weren't interested in him and got under their feet. When we were out walking in the fields near our home and encountered some, he would run towards them and they would chase him. He thought it was a great game and, luckily, he was quick and nimble enough to get out of the way of their hoofs.

Amanda and I made sure the shifts she worked at the station and the ones I worked as a surveyor were arranged in such a way that Bailey wasn't left alone during the day. But sometimes there were periods when he was on his own for a short time. A neighbour told us to that he howled when we weren't there. She wasn't complaining but, as a dog owner herself, was concerned. Next time our shifts meant that Bailey would be alone for a while, I left my phone at home with a sleep app open. It was meant to pick up and track my snoring in the night, but I reckoned it would pick up Bailey's howling too. Sure enough, when I returned home and checked it, Bailey had been howling.

It was around this time that Amanda and I started talking about getting another dog to keep Bailey company. It was just an idea we were toying with when, one afternoon, I popped out of work for some fresh air in the winter sunshine and noticed a man with a little Jack Russell. I was amazed that the dog wasn't on a lead and was obediently walking next to his owner. I thought: *That's very good.*

When I was a child, we'd had a Jack Russell and he'd been a great family dog but not very obedient. Although we loved him very much, I'd decided I'd never own a

Jack Russell. When I saw this dog walking so well without a lead I was interested. Just then, his owner ducked into a shop, and as I watched the dog, I realized that things weren't perhaps as they had first seemed.

I went over to the shop, popped inside and found the man I'd seen go in moments earlier. I approached him, 'Sorry to trouble you, but that dog outside, is he yours?'

'No,' he replied. 'He just started following me and I thought if I came inside he might go back to his owner.'

What the man hadn't figured out, which I just had, was that the dog was a stray.

I stepped back out and the little dog seemed lost and confused. He was trying to latch on to anyone walking past. When he darted into the road, I rushed after him, scooped him up and carried him back to the pavement. His heart was hammering and he was clearly very scared.

He wasn't wearing a collar so I got into my car with him and drove to a local vet, who scanned for a microchip and found the details of his owner. Immediately, she called the number registered on the database but it was unobtainable, so she sent a letter to the owner's address, saying that their dog had been found.

In the meantime, we called the dog warden, who said he'd pick him up the following day and asked if I'd keep him overnight. I had no problem with that so I took him home. I carried him through the front door as I thought it would be best to have him in my arms so Bailey didn't scare him. That was a terrible mistake.

Bailey was so intrigued that he jumped up at us over and over again to get a good look at him. The Jack Russell was terrified. I'd nicknamed him Paddy because his tail had been docked – something long outlawed in the UK but not in Northern Ireland where I suspected it had taken place.

I called Kayleigh and asked her to bring over a crate for Paddy to feel safe in, then took him upstairs to give him a bath. He was not only filthy, covered with oil, mud and other dirt, but he was a bag of bones too. As I gently washed him, I discovered he was also covered with bite marks, scratches and wounds, while his left ear was forked from a very recent tear. I wondered if the poor dog had been used in dog fights, or had led some other equally violent and miserable existence. But as I bathed and shampooed him, Paddy's shaking subsided and something wonderful happened. He climbed up the side of the bath and licked my face. It was as if he was saying: *Thank you*. It was a special moment between us and I felt a sudden connection to him.

The next day, I took Paddy to work with me, as planned, so that the dog warden and I could meet for the handover. All day long, we played telephone tag – I missed her calls, and she missed mine. When I was somewhere that would make a good meeting point, she was stuck in traffic on the other side of town.

Finally, at six o'clock, she called. 'If you're willing to house him for twenty-eight days, I can send you a form now.'

She explained that twenty-eight days was the time

frame in which we could expect him to be claimed by his rightful owners. He was a lovely dog and I thought: Who wouldn't want him? Of course his owners will come and fetch him. I agreed to keep Paddy at home with us for the time being and my next port of call was the vet. If Paddy had any problem, Amanda and I had a duty of care to get it fixed, but also we didn't want Bailey to catch any infection from him.

The vet found Paddy was full of worms so she got him started on medication and gave him an antibiotic shot, just in case.

When I took him home, we continued to use the crate and, over the course of a few days, introduced him properly to Bailey. Amanda didn't want to take them for walks together in case they had a scuffle, so I went ahead. I found they walked together beautifully, both stopping every now and then to sniff each other.

I felt even sorrier for Paddy, who had been such an unloved and abused dog, yet despite everything he had suffered, he had the biggest heart and wanted nothing more than to be loved. When I returned to the vet, she told me if Paddy hadn't been treated, the severity of the worm infestation would have killed him. In that moment, I realized something.

Even if his owners came forward, I would have real trouble giving Paddy up to them. They'd clearly neglected him and I felt angry. Amanda and I were both leaning towards keeping Paddy, and our only concern was Bailey. Would the two of them get on in the longer term? If they did, it was the perfect solution for Bailey's dislike of being alone. We'd been doing some separation-anxiety training with him and, although it was helping somewhat, we sensed he really needed a friend.

The twenty-eight days came and went, and reluctantly I called the warden.

'Nobody has come forward. Paddy is yours, if you want him.'

'He's going nowhere!' I said. 'Paddy is staying here with us.'

By now, he and Bailey had bonded and loved playing together in the garden or chasing each other around the house. Sometimes they had a bit of a spat if Paddy tried to muscle in on Bailey's toys, but mostly the days passed peacefully. That Christmas, two dogs were snoozing in front of the fire. More than wanting our attention, though, Paddy and Bailey wanted each other's. Even when they were snoozing, one would stretch out his paw to touch the other, or rest his chin on the other's leg.

Paddy was really coming into his own. He had put on weight, his coat was glossy, his eyes were bright and his stumpy tail was always going at a hundred miles an hour.

It was wonderful to see the transformation not only in him but in Bailey too. They had become best friends and what Amanda and I called tumble buddies. There was a new soundtrack to our home, with the regular crashes and bangs into furniture or kitchen cupboards as they wrestled each other to their hearts' content.

Paddy and Bailey were always either sleeping or

rolling around together. Bailey's anxiety decreased and Paddy, who was the same age as Bailey, felt he'd always been with us. He'd gone from being the dog who hadn't wanted to interact with anyone to being the bouncy little Paddy who wouldn't leave us alone.

Paddy's temperament is lovely, and whenever I remember the emaciated and scared dog I found on the road that day, I can't understand why he was ever abandoned, or put through the violent ordeal he suffered. Ultimately, of course, it was to our benefit that nobody wanted him.

Now when we walk them in the mornings, they jump into hedges, meet their friends along the way or go off together to sniff for foxes. Later we head off to work without worrying about them.

In Bailey and Paddy, Lenny's legacy lives on, and we will continue to give them all the love and attention our family has to offer.

12. From the Shadows and into the Light

It was a wet Friday night, and as the rain poured down outside, the phone began to ring.

Beside me on the settee, my husband Michael had fallen asleep so I reached to answer it. 'Hello?' I said.

'Hi, Mum,' said a voice. 'Can you come downstairs and help me bring some things up?'

I thought it was an odd request from my daughter, Claire, given that we lived in a first-floor apartment and I was seventy-six! Nevertheless, I slipped on my shoes and opened the door, ready to help as best I could.

It was then that I heard a quiet bark by my feet. I looked down and my eyes widened. There on my doorstep was a small black-and-cream Pug with a curly tail. He was sporting the biggest grin I'd ever seen and had so much energy – he was like a firework about to go off.

I wondered what was going on. Then Claire stepped out of her hiding place a few feet away and smiled.

So that's what she had been up to.

'Do you think Shadow can stay for the weekend, Mum?' she said.

My answer, of course, was yes, but before I could say anything, Shadow had galloped past me and raced – or waddled, in the way Pugs do – into the living room, jumping on every bit of furniture in sight.

I laughed as Claire enveloped me in one of her usual bear hugs. We turned just in time to see Shadow jump up on Michael's lap. He woke, confused, with a start. 'Oh! A little dog! Look, Mildred!'

But what happened next was magical. Michael's confusion softened into a beautiful smile. It was one of my favourite things about him and I loved seeing it. Sadly, for a while, his health had been deteriorating, and the cancer now had him firmly in its grip. He was growing weaker by the day. But, for a lovely moment, there was a twinkle in his eyes as he stroked Shadow.

Claire came in, pulled off her coat and slipped out of her shoes. We cut straight to the chase because Michael and I were desperate to hear about Shadow.

'Where did he come from?' I asked.

Claire, who is the chief executive of Battersea Dogs & Cats Home, said Shadow, a Pug cross, had been found wandering the streets of London, foraging in bins and rubbish before somebody had brought him to Battersea. She said: 'Mum, I know you and Dad haven't been the same since Winky died, and when I saw Shadow, I knew he'd be perfect for you.'

Winky had been our Whippet rescue that had died a few years earlier aged eighteen. We'd loved taking her for walks and had missed her terribly. Though it wasn't normal for a Battersea dog to be rehomed like this, Claire was able to make an exception for us. She knew our circumstances and how much time we had to devote to a dog, as well as the experience we'd had with Winky and all our family dogs before her. So, Claire became our own family's rehomer – even down to the home visit! And Shadow had come to see if we were all a match for each other.

'I know you've wanted a Pug for a long time,' Claire went on, 'and when I saw him out of my office window, I knew he'd be perfect for you.'

It was true. Months earlier, I'd confided in Claire that since we'd lost Winky a certain something had been missing from our lives. I had told her that I'd love a little dog to keep us company. Now, she'd delivered to us the perfect candidate to fill the empty spot in our hearts and lives.

Claire reached over and took my hand. 'But you don't have to have him if you don't feel he's the right fit for you and Dad. There are lots of animals waiting for a loving owner like you.'

'Why on earth would I say no?' I said. 'Of course we want him!'

Claire smiled and so did I. She went out to her car and brought back a new dog bed, food, toys, a collar and a lead for Shadow.

In the morning, I took Shadow to the park for a walk. People stopped to chat, and anyone who set eyes on him was immediately as smitten as I was. I could tell he would quickly become a local celebrity.

I'd learnt from friends who had them that Pugs were wilful and determined but, above all, loyal companions. They were playful, too, and very sociable. Later that day we had friends over for dinner and Shadow rushed about excitedly, saying hello to everyone, as I'd expected he would. Excitement got the better of him, and for a few minutes, he rushed around like a mad little monkey. But when he realized everyone was carrying on as normal, he calmed down, found a place by my feet and laid his head down to rest.

Next day, our son, Sean, and his little girls, Ashleigh and Trinity, came to meet Shadow. Ashleigh said: 'He's not very pretty, Grandma, but he's still quite cute, isn't he?'

And he was. Wherever we went, people wanted to stroke him or ask about his background. I told them about Battersea and how Shadow might be staying with us for good.

By now Michael was too weak to walk, but later I drove him and Shadow to the park and set up a picnic chair for Michael to sit on. Shadow raced around while Michael threw a ball for him. Before Michael had become ill, we'd both been keen walkers and had spent many a weekend wandering through the woods near our home with Winky. After so long without a dog, it felt lovely to be outside and feel the spring sunshine on our skin. Michael was glowing too.

On the Sunday evening, it was time for Claire to leave our home in the West Midlands and return to London with Shadow. During the time he'd spent on the streets, he had developed a terrible infection in his teeth and most of them were due to be removed; extensive dental work was scheduled for him.

Though we'd had Shadow only for the weekend, Michael and I were close to tears when we said goodbye to him and couldn't wait for his return.

Two weeks later, Claire called. 'Shadow is fit and ready for you. I'm bringing him home.'

The next day, Shadow was back with us, as excited to see us as we were to see him. He raced all over the flat until he ran out of steam, then sank into his new bed by the fireplace and promptly fell asleep next to Michael's armchair.

Shadow was home.

I stared at our dog and wondered how anybody could have had the heart to abandon him.

His story was a sad one: Shadow was nine years old and had never been truly cherished, despite his love of life and passion for being with people. He'd been thrown out to wander the streets of London, scavenging to stay alive. He was a lovely, gentle, kind little dog but no one had cared about or for him. His condition showed that he had never been fed a proper diet or enjoyed regimented mealtimes. His teeth were a story in their own right and among the worst the Battersea vets had ever seen. Almost every one was rotten, blackened to the root, and his breath was so bad it could have cleared a room at twenty paces. Shadow had fifteen teeth removed while the remaining few were scraped and polished to get him ready to enjoy his new life. I wouldn't have wished Shadow's history on any poor animal, but the silver lining was that he was mine. Little Shadow would never want for anything again.

Claire had brought us a rehoming pack from Battersea, with a booklet that gave details of Shadow's injections, plus all manner of advice and information. So, while Shadow snoozed, I sat back and immersed myself in all things Battersea and new dogs.

Though Michael's health was failing fast – he couldn't stand and didn't often speak – Shadow fell in love with him instantly and with all his heart. From the moment he came into our home, he developed a special bond with Michael. He would jump on to Michael's knee, plonk his bottom down and gaze up at him with those shiny brown eyes. That goofy, toothless grin made Michael smile and I often wondered if that was what Shadow was trying to do. For the first time in many months Michael felt some joy and that helped ease our pain tremendously.

Shadow certainly knew how to get things done. Every morning, I woke at seven to take him for a walk. If I was a minute late, Shadow poked and prodded me until I got up. We'd stride out for two good long walks every day, and when Michael was up to it, I drove us all to the woods near our home and set him up in his picnic chair on the grass near the car park. Shadow, already clearly a show-off who loved stopping to chat to people, ran back and forth between Michael and me. Michael would throw the ball for him when he could and that was just lovely: a time of peace and a time of happiness.

At home, Shadow basked in the late-afternoon

sunshine that flooded through our floor-to-ceiling bay window. He loved watching the world go by outside, and whenever somebody pulled into the car park outside our home, he let out a bark. I told Michael: 'Shadow would make the very best car-park attendant, don't you think?'

Michael nodded and gave a soft laugh. We had been married for fifty years and I never tired of hearing his lovely laugh.

Before he had retired, Michael had been a civil engineer, and after Claire and Sean had gone to school, I'd joined the police force, then retrained as an occupational therapist and later worked with a bereavement service, where I was the chairperson. The service had grown over sixteen years from a handful of volunteers to more than fifty counsellors, who helped give people strength and courage to cope with bereavement.

Though my work there kept me busy, the pace of our lifestyle was very different now from what it had been in previous years. That was especially so after Michael had suffered a serious stroke and then, later, the cancer. We no longer went dancing or for long walks; instead, we just enjoyed each other's company, which I didn't mind at all, but Shadow gave us both a boost.

One afternoon I noticed Michael didn't have the energy to stroke Shadow. Shadow had already sensed something was wrong and was sitting quietly beside him. I called our doctor, who arranged for an ambulance to take Michael to the local hospital. He was admitted and I visited twice a day for several weeks. Of course, dogs weren't allowed, but every day Michael said, 'How is Shadow? Where is he?'

I'd explain that he'd made some new friends in the park, or had an evening with the grandchildren, who came to our home two nights a week after school.

Then Michael said: 'I wish I could see Shadow again.'

The next day, I put Shadow into the car and drove to the hospital. When we arrived, I went around the side of the building to the window of the ground-floor ward where Michael was. I knocked on it, and when I had Michael's attention, I held Shadow up to the window. Shadow wriggled and panted in my arms as he caught his own reflection in the window but that made it all the more fun. Inside the ward, smiles raced around the faces of patients, nurses and doctors. Most importantly, Shadow brought a smile to Michael's face and that made me very happy.

Every day I returned with Shadow until, a few weeks later, it was decided Michael should be moved to a hospice.

The night before the move, we gathered at Michael's bedside and, though he was now unconscious, we all talked to him and told him the latest about the Olympics, which he had been watching keenly. I believed that, although he wasn't able to open his eyes and look at me or talk, he could hear me.

After the rest of the family had returned to their homes, I stayed with Michael and chatted to him while I put moisturizer on his hands and face. At nine p.m.,

I kissed him goodnight. 'I'll see you tomorrow,' I told him.

I went home and straight to bed, only to be woken at two o'clock by the phone ringing.

I listened to the nurse at the end of the line and I thought: *Did I hear that right?*

Michael had passed away at one forty-five a.m.

I put the phone down and my mind raced with if-onlys.

If only I'd known the end was quite so close I would have stayed the night. If only I hadn't left. If only I had stayed . . .

Sean and I went to the hospital and sat with Michael. He looked so very peaceful and I knew, after all the illness Michael had suffered, he was in a better place now.

I'd spent all those years helping others cope with grief and, now that it was upon me, I felt an odd sense of calm. Michael had always supported me in everything I had done and I knew he would be looking down on me now and looking after me.

At home, Shadow kept glancing at Michael's chair and I know he sensed something had happened because he didn't leave my side for a second. Wherever I went, he followed.

I threw myself into planning Michael's funeral to try to keep busy. It seemed odd, but planning the service and cremation Michael had said he wanted was a comfort to me.

On the morning of the funeral, I told my family Shadow and I would meet them at Sean's house when we were ready. Everyone was concerned about my being alone, and I understood that, but, for a reason I couldn't explain, I wanted to be on my own with my little boy that morning. I didn't want anyone around me, only Shadow. I knew that, as long as I had him, everything would be OK.

I got myself ready, brushed Shadow nicely and, with him sitting beside me in the car, drove to my son's house. Throughout the service, where I read from the Book of Corinthians, and the wake, Shadow stayed right by my side. Having him to stroke and cuddle was a real help.

Claire's dog, Wilma, was there too, as was Sean's. Though the day was heavy with grief, there were the inevitable moments of lightness that, mercifully, find their way into all such sorrowful occasions. Every time one of the dogs wove in and out of someone's legs or rolled over for a playful, silly moment, they prompted laughter and smiles.

That night, Shadow came to bed with me and slept on Michael's pillow.

Afterwards, I didn't let myself grieve properly – I had done so much of that when Michael had been ill – but there were days when I didn't want to get out of bed or go outside. But my lovely little dog would prod me and remind me that I still had a lot to do and walkies were at the top of the list. He knew how to get me through it.

We started walking more, and I realized that while Michael had been unwell, my pace of life had slowed down to match his although, thankfully, I was still fit and healthy. Now, with Shadow at my heels, my lifestyle was changing.

By winter, my wardrobe was filled with walking boots, coats, hats and scarves.

Every day Shadow and I went to our favourite park where we'd meet lots of friends. There was a group of local people with dogs and every afternoon, at two o'clock, we'd gather at our meeting point by the park's exercise machines. As soon as we arrived and I opened the car door, Shadow flew out and barked at the waiting gang, as if to say: *I'm back!*

While some of the ladies and gentlemen exercised on the machines, the others watched the dogs. And what a gathering it was! There were up to fourteen dogs, including two German Shepherds, two Rottweilers, one Pug, my Pug cross, two Yorkshire Terriers, four mongrels and two Poodles.

Shadow loved socializing and didn't have a problem with any of them. The only time he acted up was when he saw a black Labrador that lived in our apartment block. I couldn't figure out why because the other dog was a lovely one, but I reasoned it was something from Shadow's past. Eventually, whenever I saw the Labrador's owner, she'd point in the direction she was walking and I'd take Shadow the other way.

During the week, Shadow came with me to the offices of the bereavement service. If I was sitting behind the desk in the waiting area, he slept in his basket in a corner of the room. People waited for their appointments two or three at a time in that room.

Sometimes they'd become distressed or arrive upset. Whenever that happened, Shadow popped over and gently nudged them to stroke him. It seemed he could sense when somebody was in need and wanted to be there for them. He really was a loving little dog.

If I got up to go somewhere Shadow would come with me and often we'd encounter someone in tears. I'd stop to talk to them. They'd stroke Shadow and I'd watch as their tears slowed and their shoulders relaxed. Shadow made them feel better, just as he'd given me peace after Michael had passed.

But Shadow wasn't always an angel. He could be a bit of a monkey sometimes.

Whenever he was running about in a field on one of our walks, he found it to his advantage to stop and chat to anyone having a picnic. Once, I waited for him to come back to me, as he always did, and he returned with a pasty in his mouth.

'Shadow!' I said. 'Did you steal that?'

I found the family Shadow had been chatting with and apologized for his theft.

'Oh, he hasn't stolen it,' I was told. 'Our son dropped the pasty on the ground and we gave it to him.' I wasn't sure if it was the truth or if the family were trying to save me embarrassment, but it wasn't the only time Shadow returned to me with other people's picnic treats in his mouth. He had a habit of slipping into foraging mode so whenever he veered towards a bin or a pile of rubbish I'd guide him the other way and tell him *no*.

He learnt very quickly.

Somehow, with Shadow by my side, the summer flew by and soon the leaves had dropped, the ground had frozen and it was nearly Christmas, which had always been a special time for our family. Some people who've suffered a loss may not put up a tree, but that first year after Michael's passing, I knew he wouldn't have wanted us to miss out. So, I pulled ours out of the cupboard, and as I decorated it, I told Shadow: 'This is your first Christmas.' He watched with curious eyes as I draped the tree in tinsel and fixed colourful baubles in place. I was sure my little man understood that something magical was starting.

Michael had always loved Christmas and I was determined this year would be as special as ever. I placed flickering candles around the apartment, played Christmas carols and, slowly but surely, started to feel the warm glow of the season.

The weekend before Christmas, the entire family gathered together and with one of us on the piano, and the rest with maraccas, a drum, a tambourine or other such instruments from my granddaughters' toy box, we all sang songs and carols. It's a tradition of ours and that year Shadow watched us, fascinated. For us, that was when Christmas got under way.

Shadow and I often stayed with Sean and his wife Nicole, but I wanted us to enjoy Christmas morning at our own home. As the big day finally dawned, it was just my little boy and me. I put the radio on in the background, and as jingly music played, we had breakfast together. Afterwards, I gave Shadow his present, which

I'd wrapped in green-and-red paper. He tore it apart to find, to his joy, a squeaky meerkat.

The moment I started opening mine, he put his toy down and watched me. I was certain he knew what was happening.

Then I packed a bag and Shadow's furry bed, and drove to Sean's house. We all had a lovely day together. Sean's dog, Bentley, a rescue Pointer cross, had tinsel around his collar – even the fish had some on their tank.

We exchanged gifts and my two granddaughters sat with Bentley and helped him open his presents. Later we all tucked into a wonderful Christmas lunch. On Boxing Day, we repeated all the fun at Claire's house. There was more turkey and more laughter than you could hope for in a year. Claire's dogs, Simba, a German Shepherd, Wilma, a rough-haired Jack Russell, and Beanie, the grumpiest and probably the oldest Jack Russell in the world, Shadow and Bentley all had tinsel around their collars, and chased each other happily about, with toys and wrapping paper flying everywhere.

At lunchtime, the dogs should have known to stay away, but they couldn't resist running under the table for scraps of turkey. 'They are naughty, aren't they?' I said to Claire. 'They really shouldn't be under the table!'

She nodded, then laughed and, of course, we let them stay exactly where they were, sneaking bits of turkey to them when we each thought no one else was looking.

Shadow and I stayed with Claire for three weeks and

when we came home, after the first time I'd been away without Michael, I was glad I had Shadow with me so I wasn't coming back to an empty house on my own.

We enjoyed our meals together and in the evening, we liked to sit on the settee with the telly on or I'd read a book. Shadow sat beside me on his pillows and snoozed. Every now and then he'd throw himself against me for a cuddle and to remind me he was there. We'd got to know each other very well and could predict each other's behaviour. If I got up to go to the kitchen, I knew Shadow would come with me. When we had visitors I'd put the day-to-day sofa covers away, and Shadow would know we were about to receive guests so he'd go to his bed, like a good boy.

It didn't always work in my favour. Whenever I put a nice outfit on, he'd know he wasn't coming out with me. He'd slump in front of me, with his chin on his paws, and stare at me with those lovely brown eyes, as if to say, *I'm not coming, am I?*

He was trying to guilt-trip me and it was hard not to feel it. Still, I'd tell him, 'You'll be a good boy for Mummy. I won't be long.'

When I returned, Shadow would have turned his bed upside-down and thrown all his pillows out. He'd have had a little tantrum because he didn't like me going out without him. I came to expect it so, after a while, I accepted this was his behaviour and tidied up after him. Sometimes Shadow wouldn't talk to me for a while but he'd soon get over it.

Most places I went, Shadow came with me. He loved being in the car and seeing all my friends. One day, I put him in the car and drove to meet Claire and Wilma. We were in Biggleswade to lay a wreath at the grave of Mary Tealby, the incredible founder of Battersea Dogs & Cats Home.

Shadow wore his Battersea coat with pride and I felt fit to burst as he sat down beside the memorial and looked about him. With a dozen or so others, we paid tribute to a special lady. Claire said a few words and we said our own silent thanks to Mary for her love and devotion to animals: without her, I and several million other people, over 150 years, would never have had the pleasure of owning a Battersea animal – for the Home would not exist. It was a memorable moment and it felt wonderful to be a part of it. It was all because of Shadow that I'd even thought to join Claire on that unique trip.

Shadow came into my home that wet Friday and, ever since, he's brought me so much joy.

I honestly believe when somebody is living alone like me and still has a lifetime of love to give, it's the best thing in the world to have a little dog. I'm lucky that I have lots of friends and family, but many people don't. When you have a dog, people stop and talk to you, even if you're just sitting in the park enjoying the fresh air. I think Shadow was meant to come to me when he did. Without him, I don't know how I would have coped with losing Michael.

I know that we all have a shadow and usually we only see it in the sunshine, but my shadow has four legs, hardly any teeth and a curly tail. He's been with me through the dark times and, with his enduring love, he's brought me back to the light.

13. A Date with Santa

It was late July, and as the sun rose to its highest in the summer sky, I looked at the figure beside me and smiled. I was on holiday and my little girl was wearing an oversized sunhat and was snoozing peacefully on a deckchair. But that little girl was not my toddler daughter Lizzy: she was my West Highland Terrier, Jessie. While all the other dogs on the beach in Cornwall, our favourite holiday spot, were splashing about in the sea, Jessie refused to set foot on the sand. Instead, like a tiny human being, she sat dozing next to me on her chair.

My husband, Wayne, and our son, Matthew, arrived back from a swim and both began laughing. 'I see Jessie has the best seat, as always,' Wayne said.

Jessie was indeed a pampered pooch. Sometimes I reckoned she thought she was human. Whenever I fetched her lead for a walk, she'd go to the window and look outside. If it was sunny, she'd come to me and wait for me to clip the lead to her collar. If it was raining, she'd look at me as if to say, *I'm not going out in that*, and promptly return to her spot on the sofa.

If we did manage to get her outside, she'd sit down in the middle of the pavement when she'd had enough and refuse to budge. Even when I said, 'Come on, then, let's go home,' she wouldn't move. I'd have to pick her up and carry her or she'd have stayed out there all night!

I'd grown up with terriers and Jessie was our first family dog. She wasn't a typical terrier, though. She wasn't interested in playing and, if you threw a ball for her, or rolled it towards her to entice her to play, the look on her face said it all: *I see the ball, Mum, and I'm not interested.*

But it was all those little quirks that we loved about her, especially me, and Jessie was very much my dog. She brought so much life into our home and Matthew and Lizzy adored her.

When she was eight, I was the first to notice that Jessie was limping slightly.

I took her straight to the vet and, after many tests and scans, she was found to have lesions on her brain caused by a virus. The vet told me, 'We can manage her symptoms for now, Claire, but ultimately it will be fatal.' She would have, at best, two years. It was devastating news.

I took Jessie home and gave her the prescribed steroid medication twice a day. In time, she developed diabetes and we all learnt how to administer her injections, even Lizzy, who was eleven at the time.

Jessie never complained or flinched. Even when she starting losing motor control, she didn't whine when she slipped and cut her lip or stubbed her nose hard.

Instead, she would fall asleep on the sofa every night and wait for me to find her. We had the same routine every night. I'd say, 'Jessie, come on, girl, in your bed.'

But she wouldn't make a move towards it. Instead, she would roll on to her back and stretch out with her legs in the air. She was like a baby waiting to be picked up. Jessie stayed there until I gave in and lifted her into her bed. I was happy to indulge her.

We'd taken her in at five months old from a family who hadn't wanted her, and I'd formed an instant bond that had deepened over time. Even though she was now eleven, she was still very much my baby. We'd been lucky that Jessie was never alone for more than an hour or two. Wayne was a postman, and when he came home in the early afternoon I left for my work as a part-time administrator.

One evening, I gave Jessie her dinner and realized she couldn't chew her food. I mashed it for her and waited for her to eat but still her mouth didn't seem to be working properly. She was becoming confused, and when she began to shake, Wayne and I headed to the vet.

When he examined her, his look was grave. 'Jessie's symptoms are because of her lesions and I'm afraid she's only going to get worse.'

I said: 'Is there anything we can do?'

He shook his head.

I knew there was only one way forward but I was desperate for him to give me a different answer. 'If this was your dog, what would you do?'

'I'd have her put to sleep,' he replied. 'It's the kindest thing when she is this unwell.'

I looked at Wayne and he nodded. We had some time

with Jessie and we said our goodbyes to her. We left the clinic an hour later, and my arms felt painfully empty. I had come to the vet hoping he would help Jessie to have a little more time with us, and now I was leaving without her.

The house felt empty without her around, and I couldn't bear to pack her things away. Every time I caught sight of her little bed and pink blanket, my chest ached.

Every day when I came home from work, instead of having her little face appear behind the door as soon as I opened it, there was nothing.

I told Wayne: 'When I get home there's nobody here.'

He dealt with it as he always had – with an attempt to make me smile. 'The kids are here when you get home. Maybe we can get Matthew to run up and down the stairs for you.'

'You know what I mean,' I said.

'Of course I do, darling,' he said gently. 'So what shall we do?'

'I don't want to wait to get another dog,' I said. 'I want one now.'

'Agreed.'

We both wanted a rescue dog so I began looking at centres near our home in Essex. The only specification we had was that the dog was a terrier of some kind.

They were so full of fun, and they looked at you with such intelligence – you couldn't pull the wool over a terrier's eyes.

And I was a sucker for a sob story. If we found a dog

245

with three legs and an eye missing in the local dog rescue, I would have been lost.

A month passed and, unfortunately, there wasn't anything suitable.

As December arrived and the nights grew ever longer, we put up our Christmas tree and lit the fire. We went through the normal motions, but without Jessie wearing her Christmas jumper with a pudding on it, then huffing and puffing about the fireplace getting too warm, or ignoring the presents under the tree unless there was a treat in one, things didn't feel right.

On Christmas Eve, I hung our stockings by the fireplace, including Jessie's because I didn't have the heart to leave hers out. Then Wayne placed the final present under the tree. He turned to me and said: 'That one's for you.'

'Unless it's a dog, I don't want to know,' I said.

He smiled. 'It's best that it's not a dog because it's been wrapped for two weeks!'

Next morning, Wayne and I got up at six and Mum came over half an hour later. Before the day got under way, and hours before the kids were awake, we sat down for a cup of tea, a bacon sandwich and a catch-up.

It was our second Christmas without my dad, Albert, and the first without Jessie. We were a bit subdued. The rest of the day passed for me in a muted blur, as though I was watching everything from inside a bubble. The dull ache of reality that there was no Dad and no Jessie was kept just out of reach by the rest of the family at my side.

Everywhere I went in the house I was reminded of Jessie. The red leather armchair by the window that she would perch on to stare out into the street still had a little dip and a crease from where she'd sat. In the garden, there was a little trail carved through the grass and into the shrubs: Jessie would always run down the same path when she'd spotted a squirrel at the back.

After Christmas, I told Wayne: 'I can't take this. We have to find a dog.'

It was then that I logged on to the Battersea Dogs & Cats Home website and looked through the list of animals waiting for a home. Days later, Wayne, the kids and I went to Battersea in London. We filled out a form and had an interview with a rehomer.

I told her about our family and she had some questions too.

What sort of dog would you like? If there was a physical problem with a dog, would you be willing to take it on?

I said: 'We made provision for Jessie all of her life, and we're not scared of having to administer medicine or whatever else a dog might need. We'll take care of it, always.' Then I joked: 'He can have three legs and one eye and I'll happily take him home.'

After the interview, we were shown around the kennels to see if there might be a dog we were interested in. I was excited, wondering if I'd find that chemistry, the moment when a little dog simply jumps straight into your heart, like Jessie had. But my experience was quite different. I found it upsetting to walk around Battersea, knowing I couldn't give all those poor animals a home.

Then we spotted a Jack Russell called Duffy. She was around three years old and very timid. When we stopped by her kennel, she wouldn't leave her blanket or come towards us. I was thinking out loud when I said, 'Bless her, she doesn't look very happy, does she?'

'Let's see if we can perk her up,' Lizzy said.

The rehomer told us Duffy's profile was a good match for our family so we reckoned it was worth a meet and greet.

We were taken to a room on the first floor and waited for Duffy to be brought to us. When she arrived, it was obvious she was quite nervous and shy. She stayed close to the wall at all times and, even though she was a young dog, she wasn't at all interested in playing. In my heart, I knew Duffy wasn't right for us but I was certain she would quickly find a new home. She was young and perfect for another family.

After twenty minutes, the rehomer came back and I said, 'We all think she's beautiful, but she's not quite right for us. We'd like to go on and keep looking.'

The rehomer was very understanding. 'It's no problem. Any match has to be right for the animal and the owner.'

We returned home and I couldn't stop thinking about all the dogs we'd seen at Battersea. You had no idea what was going on in their little brains or what they were feeling while waiting for a new home. Somehow that realization made me even more determined to get a dog from there.

But I was anxious. What if Battersea thought we

were not serious about taking a dog on because we'd turned Duffy down?

Wayne reassured me. 'I'm sure the most important thing is that the dog is happy and in the right home. I promise you, Battersea will not think badly of us for wanting to wait for the right dog.'

He was right.

Weeks later, I had a phone call from Battersea. 'We have a dog that matches your profile. His name is Santa.'

I learnt that the mongrel puppy had been brought in on Christmas Eve by a member of the public who had found him wandering in the streets of London. He was between three and six months old and suffering from a skin condition that had caused his fur to fall out. The rehomer continued: 'We don't know what mix of dog Santa is for sure but he looks like a Jack Russell cross. He's been treated for his skin condition in the clinic and he's now ready for rehoming.'

The more I heard about this little puppy, the more I wanted to see him. 'Do you have a picture of him?' I asked.

She promised to text one to me. Minutes later, my mobile beeped and when the picture loaded, I smiled. Santa was sitting on a red-tiled floor and was staring innocently at the camera. He was gorgeous and there was something about his face that made my heart melt. I absolutely had to meet him.

The text below the picture read: *Let us know if you're interested.*

I texted back: *Yes please, we'd love to meet him.*

Next, I texted Santa's picture to Wayne, Matthew and Lizzy: *I've made an appointment to meet this little chap.*

I texted his picture to Mum and my sister Janet, and for the next few hours, my phone didn't stop beeping.

Oh, he's gorgeous!

What a sweetheart!

Look at that face!

When can we meet him?

Over the next week, I found myself studying that picture of Santa and trying to glean some information from it. *Was he playful? Did he look loving and caring? Would Jessie have got along with him?*

Saturday could not come quickly enough, and first thing in the morning, we all piled into the car and went to Battersea.

We entered the security gates and waited in Reception. As I watched the staff go about their business, I felt butterflies in my tummy. I was as nervous as I would be for a job interview but, rather than being worried about getting the job, I was worried that I'd fall in love with Santa but Battersea wouldn't give him to us.

I whispered my worries to Wayne, and he said: 'Don't be silly, darling. Whatever is meant to be will be. If this little boy is supposed to come home with us, he will.'

Despite his attempt to calm my nerves, my foot tapped incessantly and I didn't know what to do with my hands. I could see Lizzy was the same so I held her hand and willed things to move faster. I reckoned that, between us, our misplaced energy could have lit up Big Ben for a few hours.

Ten long minutes later, the door to the left of us opened and a member of staff appeared holding a puppy. She had Santa in her arms and his whole bottom half was moving from side to side because his tail was wagging so much.

Tears sprang to my eyes – I just had to have him.

We were taken to a room and Santa was lovely. He was running and playing, and even though he was hairless because of the skin condition he was being treated for, we barely noticed it. Ultimately, it didn't matter if he had fur or not as long as we could take him home.

For fifteen minutes we played with him, and he was as warm and loving as I'd hoped he'd be. We all got on the floor and Santa ran around us, over us and back and forth between us. The rehomer brought us a ball and some toys and left us to get to know each other.

Santa's tail did not stop wagging even though his skin still looked sensitive and his fur was only just grow-ing back. He licked our hands and offered kisses as if he'd known us for years. After ten minutes, I called my sister. 'Janet, he's so lovely, we're besotted with him.'

I could hear the smile in her voice when she said: 'I knew he would be. Enjoy every moment.'

When the rehomer reappeared, I told her: 'We abso-lutely love him.'

'Let me fetch the vet for a chat,' she said, smiling.

When she returned with the vet, Shaun, I recognized him from *Paul O'Grady: for the Love of Dogs* and he was as lovely in real life as he had been on screen. Shaun told us all about the skin condition Santa was suffering from and we learnt it was a mite problem that was passed from mum to puppy and wasn't contagious. 'It's treatable and won't be a problem now that he's on the mend.'

I was fixated with hearing as much as possible about Santa so I began asking questions. 'Do you know exactly how old he is? Or what breed cross he is?'

'We think he's between three and six months old but we can't be sure as we have no background information about him, but we do think he will be a small dog.

'As for the breed, he could be anything, but probably a Jack Russell mix. It's really hard to tell without his fur.'

Santa had only a thin smattering of fur so there was no telling if it was rough or smooth.

'But his hair will grow back in time,' the vet said. 'It's already much better than when he came in so it should be back to normal in a couple of months.'

Santa already had some white fur growing around his chin, like a little beard. It only made him more adorable.

It was so reassuring to talk to the vet and it was clear he was in no hurry to get away. Even though he must have had a thousand other things to do, he made us feel like we were the only people in Battersea. After he left, I told Wayne: 'I'm so glad we came here.'

We filled out all the relevant paperwork and were given handwritten notes from the vet about Santa's continued skin care. While we waited for him to be microchipped and given his first injections, we went into the Battersea shop and bought him a bed, toys and treats. We were giddy with excitement as we picked things out for our new little boy. With Jessie, we'd accumulated a lot of her things over time, but with Santa, we had so much fun splurging on things for him that, admittedly, we went a bit overboard.

When he was finally brought out, Santa was so happy. The staff member who handed him over to us said: 'I fostered Santa for a while. He's adorable and loves to hog the sofa. I fell in love with him and I know you will too.'

I'd known he would be perfect from the minute I'd seen his picture but hearing it from someone who had taken care of him for a few weeks meant a lot to us. 'We'll let you know how he's getting on,' I promised her.

When we got him home, I held Santa in my arms and gave him a tour of the house. I put his bed in the open-plan kitchen-diner and my eyes fell on Jessie's blanket. I picked it up and placed it in Santa's bed. I told him: 'This was your big sister's blanket and I know she would have wanted you to have it.'

Without so much as a sniff, he climbed right in and snuggled down.

While he settled in, we set about picking a new name for him. In the end, I posted a picture of him on Facebook and asked my friends: 'What should we name him?'

There were the usual replies, Max, Rex and Oscar, but nothing jumped out at me. Suddenly, something popped into my head. I said: 'What about Bertie?'

Matthew was in the other room playing on his Xbox but he shouted: 'That's a good name, Mum! He's Bertie Battersea!'

My dad was Albert but everyone had called him Bert. Bertie seemed a fitting tribute and the name stuck.

Bertie wasn't house-trained so that was our first task. Every night I put puppy mats down in the kitchen-diner where his bed was, and in the morning, I found a million pieces of cotton wool everywhere. It might have been a problem for some but I found it funny: it was the terrier nature that I'd missed having in the house.

Within three weeks, Bertie was fully house-trained. He was as bright as a button so I wasn't surprised he caught on so quickly. But whenever one of us arrived home, we had to greet Bertie on the decking because when he got excited he'd do a little wee.

Nothing was too much trouble, but one thing was bothering me. I called my cousin Pam in tears one evening. 'Bertie is perfect for us, but I feel like I'm betraying Jessie. Will I ever love Bertie like I did her?'

My cousin was sympathetic. She'd rehomed many dogs over the years and she had some words of advice. 'You will absolutely fall in love with him, but just give it a few weeks.'

Whenever I was on a break at work, I checked in on Bertie by calling or texting Wayne for updates. One day he sent me a video in reply. I clicked play and saw Bertie sitting in his bed. His tail was wagging furiously. Then Wayne's voice came on: 'Bertie,' he said slowly, 'what have you done?'

As the camera panned away from Bertie and into the kitchen, the *bomp, bomp, bomp* of Bertie's furiously wagging tail was still within earshot. When the camera focused on the kitchen, a giggle burst out of me. Everything at Bertie height had been pulled out of the cupboards and was now on the kitchen floor. There was pasta all over the lino and the bin had been tipped out. To top it off, there was cotton wool from Bertie's puppy mat. Wayne turned the camera back on Bertie and zoomed in on his face. All I could see were the whites of his eyes, and in the background, I could hear the *bomp, bomp, bomp* of Bertie's tail. Then the video cut out and I laughed till I cried.

In that moment, I realized something. I had truly and utterly fallen in love with Bertie, just like my cousin had said I would.

Every two weeks, we treated his skin and, as the vet had predicted, his fur grew back a few months later. He is mostly black but with a brilliant white apron, white paws and a white pirate beard with white eyebrows. He looks like an old dog in a young dog's body!

Even as a puppy, Bertie's big personality shone through. He was spontaneous, funny, affectionate and stubborn as anything. If you let him off the lead in the park, he shot off and only came back when he was good and ready. In so many ways, he was the opposite of

Jessie, but we all loved him just as much. Unlike his big sister, Bertie loved squeaky toys and was always desperate to play. If I was watching TV, he'd appear in front of me with his ball. Then he'd paw at my legs and nudge me till I looked at him. If I continued ignoring him, he'd stand up on his back legs and wave his paws at me. I'd tell him: 'Not now Bertie, I'm watching TV.' Then he'd drop the ball on to the sofa and stare at me. He'd stare and stare with those puppy-dog eyes until I was on my feet and in the garden.

Our garden was 140 feet long, with more land behind it, and when I threw the ball, Bertie would run down the tiny track Jessie had worn into the ground. It was comforting to me to see that: the circle of life. And, also like Jessie, when the days were hot and he needed some shade, he'd go under the low conifer where she used to lie.

Some time later, Bertie developed a benign cyst under his front leg and underwent a small operation to have it removed. The surgery was fine but, gosh, did Bertie hate wearing the 'cone of shame'! He had no sense of its size and, as he was still a puppy, bounded around the house with it on. But when the cone connected with a chair leg or the door frame, he'd bounce back with a whiny growl as if to say, *What just happened?* We took it off at dinnertime, but he soon learnt that putting pressure on the tab at the side would undo it. After three days of constantly refixing the cone over his head we decided to take it off altogether. As I did,

I told Bertie: 'You be a good boy now, Bertie, and don't touch those stitches.'

And he did exactly as he was told.

By now, it was nearly Christmas once more and, for the first time since losing Dad and Jessie, we were all looking forward to the festivities. This time when the tree went up, Bertie was all over us trying to get a look in. On Christmas Day, I pulled out a little green-and-red-striped jumper with a white fluffy trim around the edges. I put Bertie on to my lap. 'Let's see if we can get this on you now . . .'

Usually Bertie wriggled away from any clothing, but this time he held perfectly still and let me slip on his Christmas jumper. Then he hopped down, had a little shake and proudly strutted around the room. He was doing a lap of honour and everyone in the room squealed – he looked that cute.

After Christmas dinner, we opened our presents and first to get his paws on his was Bertie. He loved ripping off the wrapping paper, and when he found he had a new toy, well, there was another lap of honour with the new toy hanging out of his mouth.

That Christmas was a world away from the last two: our house was alive once more.

Now, Bertie is two years old. He has long legs, a gorgeous Jack Russell face and short, rough black fur. We think he's a Patterdale cross. Even though he's not a puppy any more, sometimes he reverts to puppy ways. The other night, Wayne came down for work in the early hours of the morning and checked in on Bertie in the dining room to find him shivering in the corner. It turned out that when we'd drawn the dining room curtain, it had covered Bertie's bed and he'd been too scared to climb in! I'd heard Wayne laughing in the middle of the night.

Now, our home is filled with laughter and warmth and so much love because of Bertie. Our family is simply not complete if we don't have a dog and I'm so pleased we turned to Battersea to help us find ours. Everyone he meets falls in love with Bertie and we're so proud of him that we post pictures of him on Twitter for his fans to see and also on the Battersea Facebook page to let them know how he's getting on.

When we went there, every member of the Battersea team was dedicated to helping us find the right dog. In Bertie, they found us the perfect match.

14. My Darling Rosie

I moved along the platform, and as the train whistled into the station, the cold air whooshing past made me shiver. Beside me, my teenagers Billie and Liam let out that sound you make when you're freezing – 'Brrrraaaaahhhhh!'

We burst out laughing and, still giggling, boarded the toasty train. Everyone else on it had had the same idea as us: they were travelling into London for the Christmas period to see their families and, again like us, they had lots of bags. After squeezing our holdalls into any space we could find overhead and under our feet, we settled in for the journey from our home in Devon. Three hours later, the train glided into Waterloo station to a flurry of activity. Some passengers were shooting out of London in the direction we'd just come from, while others were heading to the Tube to go further into town.

Our Christmas holiday was well and truly under way and we chatted excitedly as we headed to East Dulwich where my mum and dad were waiting. For many years, my parents had lived in different countries around Europe and the Middle East while my sisters and I had spread out around Britain, starting our own families and finding our way.

Now Mum and Dad had returned to London for good and were living their dream of running a bustling pub, The Rose. This Christmas was the first for many years that we would all spend Christmas together. I couldn't remember the last time I'd been so excited. It wasn't very often that I found myself with my younger sister Paula, who lived in Taunton, and Dawn, who lived in London.

As we arrived at The Rose, I slung my arms around Billie and Liam. 'Here we go!' We entered the pub, and as I took in the massive Christmas tree by the fireplace, crammed full of decorations, and the sprigs of mistletoe hanging over the bar, I smiled. This was why my kids called Mum the 'Queen of Christmas'. She loved this time of year, and everywhere I looked, I saw her handiwork – sparkly decorations and shimmering tinsel. It was like stepping into a Christmas grotto, with jingly tunes tinkling in the background perfecting the scene.

'Look at it all,' I said, squishing the kids to my sides. 'I'm half expecting Father Christmas and a bunch of elves to come running out from the bar!'

Instead of Father Christmas, another figure approached. Mum had obviously spotted me before I'd spotted her because she'd materialized out of nowhere and was now pulling us in for the tightest bear hug. She led us into the back of the pub and the stairs to the private flat we would be sharing with the rest of our family for the next ten days.

That was when I saw the latest addition to our family. 'Hello, Rosie,' I called. 'I've heard a lot about you!'

From the top of the stairs, a pair of curious eyes and a lovely soppy face stared back at me. I couldn't see Mum's new dog's wagging tail but I could hear the *thump, thump, thump* as we climbed the staircase. As we approached Rosie, who'd been named after the pub, she moved backwards a little nervously but let us stroke and greet her.

Rosie, a Staffie and Boxer cross, had been with my parents for a month but this was the first time Billie, Liam and I had met her. She followed us around as we unpacked our things and seemed happy to see new people but I could tell she was a little bit nervous of us at first. Whenever there was a loud noise or we got a bit rowdy and raised our voices, Rosie's ears would flatten against her head and her eyes would go white. We had to reassure her, and then she'd return to normal.

Once we'd all calmed down from the excitement of seeing each other, Mum explained that my sister Dawn and her boyfriend, who lived with Mum and Dad, had come up with the idea of a pub dog. They'd made some enquiries and, after meeting Rosie at Battersea Dogs & Cats Home, they'd taken her in. Now, she was living a comfortable life at the pub but things hadn't been easy for her before.

Rosie was around two years old when she was found flailing in a frozen lake by a member of the public. It appeared somebody had thrown her into the icy water, expecting her to drown, but she had clung on, despite a life-threatening and painful hernia in her diaphragm, until someone had pulled her to safety.

Mum explained: 'Rosie was very poorly by the time she arrived at Battersea. They reckon she might have been used as a bait dog or for breeding, and when she suffered the hernia and was no good to her owners any more, she'd been thrown into that freezing lake.'

'Gosh, that's so sad,' I said. 'I don't understand how anyone could do such a thing.'

Mum shrugged her shoulders, and Rosie settled next to her. 'She's so loving,' Mum said, resting her hand on Rosie's back. 'It doesn't make any sense, Maxine.'

I looked at Rosie, who was leaning against Mum. 'I guess there are people out there without any heart.'

It was amazing how resilient Rosie was, though. She seemed to be settling in so well.

We'd not had a dog in the family before so Rosie was a very exciting addition. Every now and then I'd see her and think: *Oh! A dog!* Then my brain would catch up and I'd remember she was *our* dog.

That night, a friend of mine arrived with a Christmas tree for us. I'd found it back in Devon in the charity shop where I volunteered and had asked him to bring it by car when he came to London to save me lugging it by train. I set about putting it up in the flat, and when it was done, I thought: *Crikey. That's even bigger than the one downstairs. Mum will be chuffed!*

Mum and Dad had a twenty-four-hour licence so the pub was absolutely packed till the early hours. Liam and

I helped out in the bar but Billie came down with a cold on the night we arrived. She was seventeen but I still fussed over her, tucking her under a fluffy throw on the sofa and fetching her hot drinks. I checked in on her every couple of hours, and the second time I did so, I noticed that Rosie had snuggled in next to her. She had her head on Billie's lap and Billie was stroking her. 'Aw,' I said. 'Isn't she sweet?'

'She's been stuck to me like glue all evening,' Billie croaked.

It was nice to know Rosie was keeping Billie company while the rest of us were mucking in downstairs. The pub was big and we had a kitchen, too, so there was always something to do.

I helped behind the bar with Dawn, while Mum and Dad rushed here, there and everywhere. I was a trained chef so I was in the kitchen, too. Liam popped in and out of the kitchen. He wasn't a chef but he had a real interest in cooking – I reckoned he'd inherited it from Mum and me.

As we hurried about over the next few days, I'd spot Rosie wandering around the bar. She spent most of her time upstairs but she liked to venture down and have a chat with the customers. She stopped by the tables of merry Christmas punters for a stroke or a cuddle and everybody adored her.

Rosie was so friendly and everyone who came into contact with her could tell she was a sweetheart. She'd spent 295 days at Battersea, almost ten times the average stay for a dog at the Home, and now she was surrounded by people. I could tell she loved all the attention.

Though it was hectic in the pub, Liam, Billie and I still found time to laze about, eat ridiculous amounts of chocolate and watch naff Christmas films. It was turning out to be the best Christmas we'd ever had, and it wasn't even the big day yet!

On Christmas Eve there was a brilliant atmosphere as we all donned furry hats and Christmas jumpers. The air was zinging with excitement as couples, families and groups of friends gathered in the pub for a festive drink. The beer was flowing, and every now and then, a lively group would break into a festive tune. I smiled so much that my cheeks ached. For as long as I could remember, Christmas had been a massive deal in our family. Anything to do with Christmas, we had it, from three types of stuffing to crackers and furry hats. When I'd had children, I'd made sure it was the same for them. I loved the magic and mystery but the kids had a funny theory about the most famous man on the planet. When they were little, I'd ask them: 'Is Father Christmas real?'

They'd shout: 'Yes!'

Then I'd say: 'Who is Father Christmas?'

The reply was always the same: 'NANNY!'

Now, the kids were grown-up and, still, Mum made sure the magic remained.

On Christmas Day, we followed the usual tradition. We got up early and, still dressed in our pyjamas, gathered in the living room. We had a cup of tea, then Mum and I disappeared downstairs into the kitchen. We returned half an hour later with platefuls of scrambled egg, smoked salmon and bottles of Bucks Fizz. That was the way our Christmas Day had always begun.

Then we'd nominate a person to hand out the presents one by one. Usually it was Paula, but she hadn't arrived yet so Liam was happy to step up to the plate. It was only ten o'clock and already we were giddy with the festivities: Billie was wearing three Christmas hats, one on top of the other. Liam handed out our presents and we opened them and showed them to everyone.

We'd remained in our pyjamas because we didn't know what new clothes we'd be getting, and luxuriated in this family time because, later on, we'd be opening the pub to customers. It was going to be a busy day.

Next, we got dressed in our smartest outfits, including any new bits we'd received, because that was what we always did, and went downstairs to open up. By midday, while the rest of the family were behind the bar, Mum and I were in the kitchen preparing our family's Christmas dinner. It was going to be one heck of a feast. We'd have sixteen relatives and friends later so we cooked two huge turkeys, with three different stuffings: sage and onion, chestnut, sausage and apricot. There were six different vegetables, and pan after pan of crispy roast potatoes. Every now and then, Rosie would appear at the kitchen door, which we'd blocked with a baby gate, and stare longingly at all the food. It smelt delicious to us so only God knows how Rosie's nose was coping with the aromas.

Behind her, the pub was crammed full of punters with Christmas hats and the radio playing all the best-loved tunes.

At three, we served the last drinks, then pushed four tables together and set them for dinner. There were decorations, crackers, and everybody had a name card with a lottery ticket tucked inside for good luck in the New Year.

Mum and I served the food, and Rosie milled around the edges, waiting for a bite of something. We treated her to scraps of turkey and she looked in doggy heaven. She had made herself right at home, as if she'd been with us for years, not weeks.

After dinner, we pulled our crackers, told terrible jokes and laughed the afternoon away. When we were done, two of Mum's staff came in to open up the bar so that we could, as a family, retire upstairs to enjoy the rest of our evening.

Rosie settled into her bed with her new reindeer blanket and the toys she'd been given for Christmas, while we found a spot on the sofa or a chair to laze on and watch TV. We shared bags of sweets and revelled in how lovely it was for everyone to be together. It was such a rarity. From time to time Rosie would get up and sofa-surf, seeking love and kisses or just to sit next to someone new.

Days later, Billie, Liam and I were on our way home. I was used to spending time away from my family, but this Christmas had been so special that I didn't want it to end. We stood outside The Rose for ages, saying goodbye, then chatting, saying goodbye again, then talking.

Eventually I said: 'We're going to miss the train at this rate!' We laughed, said our final goodbyes and got into a taxi. I knew if I'd turned round one more time, I'd have seen tears in their eyes, just like the ones I had in mine.

We returned to Devon and I talked to Mum every couple of weeks for a catch-up.

When she called in February I knew instantly that something was wrong. 'What is it, Mum?' I asked.

'Something's come up for your dad and me. It's the opportunity of a lifetime.'

'Well, what is it?' I said.

'We've been offered the chance to run a marina in the Bahamas, complete with bar and restaurant.'

'Great,' I said. 'Congratulations!'

There was a silence at the end of the line, and then I twigged why. 'What will you do with Rosie?'

Mum explained that Dawn and her boyfriend would be moving into shared accommodation and were heartbroken that they couldn't take her with them. 'I thought we were going to be in this pub for good, but living in the Bahamas has always been our dream and this job has come out of the blue from an old contact of ours. I don't think your father and I can pass it up. I wondered if you would take Rosie for a couple of months while we get settled.'

I'd never had a dog before. Was this a good idea?

On the other hand, I didn't work so I had time to devote to looking after Rosie and I knew the kids would be pleased.

Maybe it wasn't such a bad idea after all.

'OK,' I said. 'I'll have to check with the landlord that I can have a dog, but otherwise I'm happy to take her in.'

Mum was so relieved. 'I know you'll take good care of her. Besides, I'll be much happier knowing Rosie's staying with a family member she's already met.' After a pause, she added: 'We'll come up with a plan for the long term.'

That day, I cleared the idea with my landlord, and when he gave me the go-ahead, I told the kids the news. Billie was chuffed. 'I can't wait!' she said.

Liam was happy too, but he had one stipulation: 'I'm not taking her for walks, Mum. I can't handle picking up her poo.'

That made us all laugh.

'Don't worry,' I said. 'I'll be the one walking her.'

Mum and Dad's move to the Bahamas was imminent so, two weeks later, they drove down with Rosie. She rushed to me in an excited blur as soon as the door opened. Mum and Dad had brought with them a box of her things, including her bed, toys and food. I put them inside and we set off for the local pub.

We had lunch there and chatted for a couple of hours. When it came time to say goodbye to Rosie,

Mum got very upset. I could understand why. I'd formed a bond with Rosie over just ten days. She had been with Mum and Dad for months. Mum said a tearful goodbye to me and we hugged each other tightly. Then she dashed to the car to have a sob in private.

Dad wasn't in such a rush. He was his usual, cool self and gave Rosie a pat on the head. 'Bye, Rosie. Bye, girl.'

As he straightened and came to hug me, I could see his eyes were filled with tears.

Dad was an ex-Marine and I reckoned he didn't want to admit Rosie had got to him. Even though his voice didn't waver, his face gave him away. It was clear Rosie had had an effect on him, too.

After I'd waved them off and watched their car pull away, I took Rosie's lead and we strolled home. That night, we spoilt her with treats, cuddles and lots of reassurance but, like the brave girl she was, Rosie took it all in her stride.

Mum called all the time to check on her and I reassured her that Rosie was doing well. Every morning I snapped on her Battersea lead and took her to the beach near our home in Paignton, Devon. In the winter, it's open to dogs so I was able to let Rosie off the lead. I was a bit nervous at first and Rosie was unsure of the sand squidging beneath her paws and the crashing of the waves. She stuck close to me and then, after a few minutes, she shot off!

Rosie ran and ran and ran. She chased the seagulls and splashed about in the sea and I smiled to see her having so much fun. Eventually, she returned to me, looking very pleased with herself. *Did you see me, Mum? That was the best thing ever!*

Everywhere I went people stopped me to talk about Rosie. 'Isn't she beautiful?' they'd say. 'What a gorgeous girl.'

I'd tell them about her sad past and they'd gasp. Then I'd tell them the amazing job the Battersea vets had done, fixing Rosie's hernia and nursing her back to health.

Billie loved having Rosie around and the two of them had a special bond. Rosie was so loving, kind and gentle, like Billie. They spent a lot of time cuddling up together, and when Billie was nearing the house, Rosie would be waiting for her by the front door.

Liam was the one to roll around on the floor with Rosie, playing rough and tumble with her. It was the only time she ever growled, even playfully, and I reckoned Liam was Rosie's secret favourite visitor.

It was no surprise that we all reached the same conclusion: Rosie was staying with us for good. I told Mum our decision and, though she was sad for herself, she agreed it was probably best for Rosie.

I'd never thought of having a dog before, but now that I had one, I wished I'd known years earlier what having a dog would do for me. If I had known that the anxiety and depression I'd suffered for so long would ease with a dog in the house, I would have searched for one like Rosie to call my own. For so many years, even leaving the house had been a big deal for me. I'd had to psych myself up to go to the shop and buy some milk. Often, the anxiety had consumed me, leaving me trapped and alone, unable to go out or complete the simplest of tasks. I'd hated going out by myself or having to talk to people I didn't know. With Rosie around, my life changed.

Every day, Rosie got me up and out, chatting to strangers and taking long walks by the sea. It was cathartic in so many ways and, before I knew it, I wasn't nervous about going outside any more. It boiled down to one very important factor: with Rosie, I no longer had to go out alone. She became my best friend and, the more time that passed, the more I felt as though it had been written in the stars for Mum and Dad to get that amazing job abroad and for Rosie to become mine. All the planets had aligned, and life had led Rosie to me.

Before she'd come to stay, I'd never understood the bond a person can share with their dog, or why someone might need a week off work if their dog passed away, but now I understood it totally. Rosie felt like my third child. Before I had her, I hadn't known that a relationship like mine and Rosie's could exist between a human and an animal.

I found myself talking to Rosie, and I was certain she understood. Every morning, she somehow knew if we'd go out or if I'd do the housework first. As soon as the thought came to me that this would be a good time to head out for a stroll, Rosie would charge around the house in a hyper mood and shake her lead off its hook in the kitchen.

Soon after Rosie's arrival, I made a decision that I'd been shying away from for a long time. I went to my local estate agent and said: 'Can you find me a house with a big garden? It's time for a change.'

He booked me in for several viewings, but it was a house in the town centre that caught my eye. As soon as I opened the kitchen door and stepped into the back garden, I thought: *Rosie will love this.* So, we moved just a few minutes away to that house with a wonderful garden. It was near the park and Rosie loved the duck pond so much that she'd race around it every time. She made quite a name for herself.

When locals spotted us on the beach, they'd point to Rosie and ask: 'Is that the loony from the park?'

I'd laugh. 'That's the one.'

It seemed to me that Rosie had come into my life at just the right time. Billie and Liam were in their late teens, busy working and seeing their friends. I'd never really stopped to think what life would be like without them around, and besides it being a lot tidier, it was much quieter too. Without Rosie, I don't know what I would have done.

One day, Rosie seemed subdued and kept shaking her head. I took her to the vet, who diagnosed an ear infection. Over a year or so, the infection returned several times and further investigation showed Rosie had a benign lump in her left ear, which was causing the repeated attacks. She had surgery to remove the diseased section of her ear canal, and returned home with a surgical collar. With her head and neck partially shaved, I noticed scars on her ear and scalp that had been previously hidden under her fur. It broke my heart to know that Battersea's theory about Rosie having been a bait dog with others set on her, was in all likelihood, with the evidence before me, correct.

No wonder she hated it when I had a row with the kids, as you inevitably do with teenagers. If we raised our voices Rosie's ears would flatten against her head and she'd cower away from us. I knew now that the shouting must have triggered memories of her former life. It had been hard to live with the idea that she had had a tough time before she'd come to us and now, looking at the marks on her bare skin, even harder to know that those awful things had indeed happened to her.

But what could we do? I was just grateful that she was with us now and living a peaceful and comfortable life.

Time passed, her fur grew back and the infections did not return. The following Christmas, the kids and I were at home, just the three of us and Rosie. It was nothing like the extravagant hoo-ha we'd had in the pub, but it was just as special. We all wore our Christmas hats and Rosie donned a pair of felt antlers. Every time I looked at her with them on, I burst out laughing. What a sight we were!

On Christmas Eve, my best friend came over, and when he placed our presents under the tree, he made the mistake of touching one of Rosie's. I'd wrapped it up and placed it there, hoping Rosie wouldn't twig what was waiting for her, but as the present let out a loud squeak, she rushed over.

The cat was well and truly out of the bag.

Rosie knew it was hers and she pressed it with her nose. SQUEAK!

She looked at me, eyes frantic. *Mum! Mum! I know it's mine, I know it's mine, I have to have it, I have to have it!* She came to me, then ran back to the toy and whined. *I KNOW IT'S MINE! I WANT IT! GIVE IT TO ME!*

It was too much delirium to tolerate so I gave it to her. She ripped off the paper and held the toy in her mouth. Then she set to work. Less than a minute later, the plastic was destroyed and the squeaker lay chewed to pieces on the floor. Rosie was looking chuffed with herself.

Now we've had Rosie for two and a half years and the kids idolize her. But my relationship with her is on a totally different level. She is constantly by my side and I never have to do anything on my own. She is my best friend and the most loyal girl I could ask for.

Having a dog is a huge responsibility, and not one to be taken lightly, but the change I feel inside me because of her is worth every moment I spend planning our days or taking her out.

If Fate hadn't brought us together, I don't think I would ever have thought to get a dog, but I'm so glad I did. I'm her mummy now and she's as content as I am. All Rosie wants in life is human company, and I'll give her that always because the companionship she has brought me means so much. She is always with me at home, and when she's not right beside me, I can hear the pitter-patter of her feet in the kitchen, or her snoring and snuffling in her bed. Knowing she is in the next room brings me so much comfort, and with Rosie around, I never feel lonely.

In the first part of her life, Rosie didn't have constant love – if any at all – but now I make sure she feels unconditional love and has the security and safety she lacked before. That's the best thing I can offer her in return for her being my best friend.

He just wanted a decent book to read ...

Not too much to ask, is it? It was in 1935 when Allen Lane, Managing Director of Bodley Head Publishers, stood on a platform at Exeter railway station looking for something good to read on his journey back to London. His choice was limited to popular magazines and poor-quality paperbacks – the same choice faced every day by the vast majority of readers, few of whom could afford hardbacks. Lane's disappointment and subsequent anger at the range of books generally available led him to found a company – and change the world.

'We believed in the existence in this country of a vast reading public for intelligent books at a low price, and staked everything on it'
Sir Allen Lane, 1902–1970, founder of Penguin Books

The quality paperback had arrived – and not just in bookshops. Lane was adamant that his Penguins should appear in chain stores and tobacconists, and should cost no more than a packet of cigarettes.

Reading habits (and cigarette prices) have changed since 1935, but Penguin still believes in publishing the best books for everybody to enjoy. We still believe that good design costs no more than bad design, and we still believe that quality books published passionately and responsibly make the world a better place.

So wherever you see the little bird – whether it's on a piece of prize-winning literary fiction or a celebrity autobiography, political tour de force or historical masterpiece, a serial-killer thriller, reference book, world classic or a piece of pure escapism – you can bet that it represents the very best that the genre has to offer.

Whatever you like to read – trust Penguin.